Moto...
Offen...
Handbook

Motoring
Offences
Handbook

What to do if you drive into trouble

J. B. GRAY

PIATKUS

Contents

Introduction   1

Part I   The Legal Framework   7

1 The Motorist and the Police   9
2 Summonses and Charges   26

Part II   The Offences   39

3 Offences and Likely Penalties   41
4 Summary Offences Which Are Not Endorsable   49
5 Summary Offences Which Are Endorsable   64
6 Motorway Offences   106
7 Alcohol-related Offences   119
8 Either Way and Indictable Offences   144

Part III   The Charge and Afterwards   161

9   Legal Advice   163
10 Guilty Pleas   173
11 Sentences and Orders   202
12 Appeals and Applications   226

Glossary of Terms   232
Common Abbreviations   236
Table of Offences   238
Index   241

Introduction

Each year, over a million motorists are charged with motoring offences and dealt with either by way of a fixed penalty or by the courts. The vast majority of those convicted are fined and may have their driving licence endorsed, depending on the offence. A not inconsiderable number are disqualified from driving for periods from a few days to a number of years. Some even go to prison...

This book is intended as a guide to persons charged with one or more motoring offences. It cannot be exhaustive but it takes a close look at the most common offences – those accounting for 99 per cent of the work of the courts. It details defences and penalties on conviction. It advises the reader of procedures before magistrates' courts.

It is intended for the average motorist, the responsible driver who, nevertheless, whether through ignorance of the law (and the law is not always what you might believe), a momentary lapse of concentration or sheer mental aberration, commits or is alleged to have committed an offence.

If you do commit an offence, this book will not 'get you off' but it will advise you, the reader, what to do – and what, very definitely, not to do. Through learning something about the system and how it works, you may be able to limit the damage.

A WORD ABOUT THE HIGHWAY CODE

When did you last read a copy of the Highway Code? The chances are that it was before you took your driving test when, for the benefit of the examiner, you memorised (and, having passed, promptly forgot) stopping distances, maximum speed limits, the meaning of the more obscure road signs and markings etc.

The 1993 edition of the Highway Code contains much information that is essential to the motorist. It sets out rules designed to prevent accidents, to avoid serious injury and to save lives. Most motorists obey those rules, but some do not. For the latter, Parliament has passed laws describing certain offences and prescribing the penalties available to deal with offenders.

Even the most experienced motorist would benefit from reading a copy of the Highway Code. Buy a copy and refresh your memory about the rules. Avoid committing offences through ignorance of the law.

HOW TO USE THIS BOOK

A busy court office deals with hundreds of enquiries from defendants each week. The most frequently asked questions are:

- Will I have my licence **endorsed?**

Key Terms

■ **Endorsement** The annotation of your driving licence with penalty points

- Am I likely to be disqualified from driving?
- Do I have to attend court?
- Should I plead guilty or not guilty?
- How much am I likely to be fined?

Chapter 1 of this book looks at **fixed penalties**, while Chapter 2 covers **summonses** and **charges**. A quick reference to the most common offences is provided in tabular form in Chapter 3 and, for convenience, these tables are repeated at the end of the book. Refer to these tables and you will see whether or not a particular offence is endorsable and, if so, with how many penalty points. You will see at a glance whether or not a conviction is likely to result in a period of disqualification from driving.

The most common offences are described in detail in Chapters 4 to 8. What must the prosecution prove if you are to be convicted? Is it possible that you may have a defence to the charge? Should you plead not guilty or guilty? Should you consult a solicitor?

You should be aware that a great many defendants consult a solicitor either needlessly or prematurely and that many who would have benefited from the advice of a solicitor fail to see one.

The vast majority of motoring offenders are dealt with by way of a fine. The maximum fine is set by statute, e.g. Level 2, Level 3 etc. These levels reflect the seriousness with which the offence is regarded. If you are to be dealt with by

---

Key Terms

■ **Fixed penalty** Provides an opportunity to have the matter dealt with other than by a court ■ **Summons** The document which begins most court proceedings ■ **Charge** An alternative to a summons usually used for the more serious offences

way of a fine, how do you persuade the court to fine you as little as possible?

A court has the power to impose a penalty greater than a fine upon conviction for one of the more serious offences. It may impose a community sentence (a probation order, a community service order or a combination of the two). Again, you will see from the tables whether or not such a penalty is a possibility.

What is involved in a probation order, a community service order or a combination order? What is likely to happen if you do not consent to such an order being made or if you break any of the conditions of the order, and under what circumstances are you at serious risk of a prison sentence? See Chapter 8.

There are offences for which you may be tried either before a magistrates' court or before a judge and jury at a Crown Court, and there are offences for which you may only be dealt with by a Crown Court. Given the option, should you prefer to be dealt with by a magistrates' court or a Crown Court? What factors should influence your decision? You will still have to appear before a magistrates' court on a number of occasions and Chapter 8 describes the procedure whereby you are committed to a Crown Court.

If you intend to plead guilty, do you have to attend court? A summons alleging one of the less serious offences will often be accompanied by a form giving you the option of pleading guilty in absence. What should you write to the court? What are the extenuating circumstances which may persuade the court to impose a lesser penalty? Examples of what you should and should not write are given in Chapter 10.

If you are confident that you have a defence to a charge and intend to plead not guilty, you will have to attend court. The fact that you cannot afford to pay a solicitor to defend you is not a good reason for pleading guilty: you should defend yourself. How do you go about that? What assistance is available? Court procedure is outlined in Chapter 10.

There are circumstances in which you may be ordered to attend court even though you intend to plead guilty to the charge or charges. You may, for example, be charged with one of the more serious offences for which disqualification from driving is compulsory, or an offence punishable by a term of imprisonment. Where this is not the case, you may be ordered to attend court for consideration of disqualification either for the offence or under the **totting-up** provisions (see Chapters 9 and 10). Your chances of avoiding disqualification may not be good but you should still make every effort to persuade the court either not to disqualify you or to disqualify you for as short a period as possible.

There are limited circumstances in which a court may be persuaded not to endorse your driving licence with penalty points or not to disqualify you from driving, even though such a penalty is mandatory. Known as **special reasons**, these may only be argued if you are present in court (see Chapter 8).

Charged with a serious offence, you may find yourself in custody. What should you do? Under what circumstances will **bail** be granted? See Chapter 11.

Chapter 12 deals with appeals and applications. You have the right of appeal to a Crown Court against a decision of a magistrates' court. You may appeal against conviction and you may also appeal against sentence. But is such

---

Key Terms

■ **Totting up** The adding together of the number of valid penalty points on your driving licence ■ **Special reasons** Reasons special to the circumstances of the offence which allow a court a discretion not to endorse or not to disqualify ■ **Bail** Release from custody with a duty to surrender to a court at a later date

an appeal necessarily a good idea? As for applications, one of the most common is an application to remove a disqualification (usually imposed for an alcohol-related offence) after two years of the period of disqualification have elapsed. How is this done? What must you show in order to maximise your chances?

In this book you will find the answers to all these questions and more. Charged with an offence, look it up in the tables, then find the page on which the offence is examined in detail. A glossary of terms, together with a list of common abbreviations, appears at the end of the book.

PART I

The Legal Framework

The Motorist and the Police

You must stop your vehicle when required to do so by a police officer in uniform. The police have extensive powers to stop vehicles using public highways and roads in the UK. These extend from random searches to specific reasons. Most usually you will have been stopped because the police officer suspects that you have committed an offence.

YOUR DRIVING DOCUMENTS

If you are the driver of a vehicle stopped by a police officer, the officer will almost certainly wish to see your driving documents, i.e. your driving licence and certificate of insurance. You will also have to produce, if relevant, the vehicle's Ministry of Transport (MOT) certificate. If you do not have these documents with you, you will be issued with an HORT 1, requiring you to produce them at a police station of your choice within seven days. Fail to do so and you commit an offence.

Are you sure you know where your driving documents are? Are they up to date? For example, have you changed your address or your name and failed to notify the Driver Vehicle Licensing Agency (DVLA)? Incidentally, if you do

HO/RT 1
THIS FORM SHOULD BE PRODUCED WITH YOUR DOCUMENTS

(Driver/Passenger/Other)   *(SEE EXPLANATORY NOTES OVERLEAF)*   Date of Birth

Surname

Forenames

Address

Post Code

Location of Stop/Incident	Time	Date

Location of requirements to produce *(if different)*	Time	Date

V R M		Manual	Motorway	L Plates
		Yes☐ No☐	Yes☐ No☐	Yes☐ No☐

Make	Passengers	Yes☐ No☐
Type/cc/ mass	Driver-Supervised	Yes☐ No☐
Use	No. of Seats	
Class/ Category	Reason for stop: Check☐ Offence☐ Accident☐	

DOCUMENTS TO BE PRODUCED   *(See explanatory notes overleaf)*

Check only   1☐ 2☐ 3☐ 4☐ 5☐ 6☐ 7☐ 8☐ 9☐ 10☐

Record details   1☐ 2☐ 3☐ 4☐ 5☐ 6☐ 7☐ 8☐ 9☐ 10☐

Police Station where document(s) to be produced ....

Forward HO/RT 2 to 'Officer in Charge'; Police Station ....

Fax No.   Post Code

Issued by (Print) .... No. |___| Station |__| Div ....

Signature ....   ROADSIDE REPORTED   Yes☐ No☐

Received a copy of this form ....   Motorist's Copy

DOCUMENTS

1 **Licence: Drivers**

(Failure to produce the required document personally at the specified police station within 7 clear days may render you liable to prosecution. A current Driving Licence Receipt may be produced if Driving Licence has been surrendered on receipt of Fixed Penalty Notice.)

2 **Licence: HGV/LGV**

3 **Certificate of Insurance**

4 **Test Certificate**

5 **Goods Vehicle Plating/Test Certificate**

6 **Driving Instruction Certificate/Licence**

7 **Licence: PSV/PCV Drivers**

(Failure to produce the required document(s) at the specified police station within 7 clear days may render you liable to prosecution. Documents (2) and (7) must be produced personally.)

8 **Vehicle Registration Document**

(The owner of the vehicle shall produce the above document at any reasonable time. It MAY be produced at a specified police station.)

9 **Seat Belt Exemption Certificate**

(To avoid prosecution for an offence of not wearing a seat belt a certificate of exemption should be produced to the specified police station within 7 clear days.)

10 **Other Documents (Specify)**

send your driving licence to the DVLA, keep a photocopy.
Occasionally, driving licences do get lost.

Tens of thousands of motorists a year are convicted and
fined for failing to produce documents. If you keep your driving licence, certificate of insurance and MOT certificate
with you whenever you drive, you cannot commit an offence
of this nature. However, do not keep your vehicle's registration document in the vehicle in case of theft.

VEHICLE CONDITION

As well as asking to see your driving documents, a police
officer is entitled to examine your vehicle for defects. The
officer will take a close look at the tread pattern on your
tyres, ask you to turn on the lights and take a look at the
exhaust system etc. If the officer believes that your vehicle is
defective in some way, you may be reported for a summons,
but it is more likely that you will be issued with a notice
under the Vehicle Defect Rectification Scheme.

The Vehicle Defect Rectification Scheme (VDRS)

A **VDRS** notice requires you to present the vehicle for inspection by a garage participating in the scheme. If the garage is
satisfied that the fault no longer exists, the garage will stamp
your notice. You must take the stamped notice to a nominated
police station within 14 days from the date it was issued.

Key Terms

■ **VDRS** A scheme whereby a motorist is given an opportunity to put right vehicle defects without penalty

CONSTABULARY

Vehicle Defect Form

(Driver/Passenger/Other)   *(SEE EXPLANATORY NOTES OVERLEAF)*

Surname

Forenames

Address

Post Code

Location of Stop/Incident | Time | Date

V
R
M

Make

Type/cc/
mass

DEFECTS   **CLASSIFICATION: CAR/VAN/M.CYCLE**   **OFFENCE CODE**

1.

2.

3.

4.

Issued by
(Print)   No.   Station   Div.

Signature   ROADSIDE REPORTED   Yes ☐   No ☐

Take advantage of this scheme and there will be no penalty.

A YOUNG man was given a VDRS notice for a faulty exhaust system. Either he couldn't afford to have it repaired or, unlike the local residents, he quite enjoyed the sound it made. A summons was issued. He was convicted and had to pay a fine plus prosecution costs. Two days after his court appearance he was stopped and given another VDRS notice.

Note that the VDRS notice is issued to the person using or driving the vehicle. The defect is the responsibility of that person and it is he or she who will receive a summons if any repairs are not carried out. So, if you drive a vehicle belonging to someone else, have a good look at it first.

Depending on the reason why the police officer stopped your vehicle in the first place, there may be a number of options.

1. The officer may decide that no offence has been committed.

2. You may simply be warned and allowed to continue your journey.

3. If the officer believes that the vehicle is defective in some way, you may be issued with a VDRS notice or reported for a summons.

4. If the officer believes you have committed a moving traffic offence, you will either be issued with a **fixed penalty** notice or reported for a summons.

Key Terms

■ **Fixed penalty** Provides an opportunity to have the matter dealt with other than by a court

5. If a serious offence is suspected, you may be arrested and taken to a police station.

If the police officer has a number of options, your attitude will be important. The more helpful and reasonable you are, the more reasonable he or she is likely to be. Be obstructive, suggest that the police would be better employed catching burglars, and you are likely to find the officer less than sympathetic.

A VDRS notice will prove less expensive than a fixed penalty notice. A fixed penalty notice will prove less expensive than a summons. Given the opportunity, you should take advantage of either of the first two options.

FIXED PENALTY NOTICES

The notice must give particulars of the alleged offence, the period within which further proceedings concerning this matter cannot be instituted, the amount of the fixed penalty and the address to which payment must be made. Fixed penalty notices are most commonly issued for one or more of the following offences.

Offences which are **not endorsable**:

exhaust emission offences

helmet, no safety helmet

lighting offences

Key Terms

■ **Endorsement** The annotation of your driving licence with penalty points

ownership, not notifying change

ownership/driver, failing to provide details of

most parking offences

seat belt offences

stopping on a clearway

stopping on the hard shoulder of a motorway.

Offences which are **endorsable:**

defective tyre

driving not in accordance with a licence

leaving a vehicle in a dangerous position

pedestrian crossing offences

speeding, exceeding the speed limit

traffic lights, failing to comply with

police/traffic signs, failing to comply with

using a vehicle in a dangerous condition

all the motorway offences described in Chapter 6, except stopping on the hard shoulder (above).

A fixed penalty notice may be issued by a police officer or a traffic warden and may either be handed to you in person or affixed to your vehicle.

You have 28 days either to pay the fixed penalty or to advise the Fixed Penalty Office that you wish to have the matter dealt with by a court.

The latter is an option that you should not even consider unless:

● you are confident that you have a defence to the charge; or

- the offence is endorsable and you wish to put forward **special reasons** for not endorsing.

In any other circumstances you are well advised to pay the fixed penalty, because if the matter is dealt with by a court, you are likely to have to pay a substantially greater fine plus prosecution costs.

Worse, where the offence is endorsable and the number of penalty points is variable (e.g. speeding, where the number of penalty points that may be ordered is any number from three to six), the Fixed Penalty Office will endorse your licence with the minimum number of points. A court, on the other hand, may (and probably will) order more.

You will not be able to take advantage of a fixed penalty for an endorsable offence if you are unable to produce your driving licence or if the details on it are incorrect (e.g. if you have changed your address and failed to notify the DVLA). If you are going abroad on holiday or on business, you may not be able to take advantage of a fixed penalty because you are not able to surrender your driving licence. You will require your driving licence if you plan to hire a car.

Inevitably, you will receive a summons. You should make it clear to the court that you were offered the option of a fixed penalty and give the reason why you were not able to take advantage of that option. In these circumstances, you may be able to persuade the court to impose a fine no greater than the fixed penalty and to endorse your licence with no more than the minimum number of penalty points.

Key Terms

■ **Special reasons** Reasons special to the circumstances of the offence which allow a court a discretion not to endorse or not to disqualify

FIXED PENALTY NOTICE   Sub Div...............

PART 1   (NON ENDORSABLE OFFENCE)

On [   ] from [   ] to/ at [   ] hrs

in [   ]

a vehicle, Registration No. [   ]

Make..........................Model...........................Colour............................
which you were driving/riding/using/ in which you were a passenger/which was
unattended, was seen in circumstances which gave me reasonable cause to believe that
the offence indicated below was being or had been committed.

Offence Code [   ] ....

....

No [   ] Signed..

PART 2   **PAYMENT SLIP**

Sur-
name

Fore-
names

Address

Post-
code [b   ]   **N**

The Fixed Penalty payable is **£20** and
you may now either:
(i) Pay the penalty in full within **28** days
    in which case the Police will take no further action in respect of this offence.
or (ii) Request within **28** days that the matter be dealt with by a Court.
                    (SEE NOTES OVERLEAF)

To: The Clerk to the Justices, Fixed Penalty Department

I enclose £20 as payment of the fixed penalty for the offence mentioned in
Part 1 of this notice.

EXPLANATORY NOTES

A. IF YOU WISH TO PAY THE PENALTY
You should use Part 2 of this Notice overleaf, to accompany payment.
Payment may only be made, by post, to the address shown overleaf.
Cheques, Postal Orders or Money Orders should be crossed and made payable to The Clerk to the Justices. If you wish to pay by cash this must be sent by Registered Post.

B. IF YOU WISH TO BE DEALT WITH BY A COURT
You should complete Part 3 below and send it to The Officer in Charge, Central Fixed Penalty Office at the address shown, within **28** days.

WARNING

IF, WITHIN 28 DAYS, YOU DO NOT PAY THIS FIXED PENALTY OR REQUEST THAT THE MATTER BE DEALT WITH BY A COURT THE POLICE MAY APPLY FOR THE £20 PENALTY PLUS AN ADDITIONAL £10 TO BE REGISTERED AGAINST YOU AS IF IT WERE A FINE FOLLOWING CONVICTION

PART 3
To: The Officer in Charge, Central Fixed Penalty Office

* Delete whichever is not applicable
* (i) I am the person named on the Fixed Penalty Notice
* (ii) I was the driver at the time the Notice was fixed to the vehicle and I wish to be dealt with by a Court for the alleged offence to which this Notice refers.

Signed.....................................Date.............................

Surname..

Forenames...

Address..

....
(Block Letters Please)

Fixed Penalty Notices Handed to You in Person

A police officer may issue you with a fixed penalty notice for a number of offences, some of which are endorsable, e.g. exceeding the speed limit, and some of which are not, e.g. failing to wear a seatbelt. If the alleged offence is endorsable, the police officer may only issue a fixed penalty notice if you have your driving licence with you and if, having examined it, the officer is satisfied that endorsement with the relevant number of penalty points will not make you liable for disqualification under the totting-up provisions. If the officer is satisfied in that respect, you will be required to surrender your licence to the officer, who will issue the notice.

If you do not have your driving licence with you, you will be required to produce it at a police station of your choice within seven days. When you do so, provided you are not liable for disqualification as above, you will again be required to surrender your licence and the fixed penalty notice will be issued.

If it is clear, either to the police officer at the scene or to the person to whom you produce your licence at the police station, that endorsement with penalty points will bring the total number of points on your licence to 12 or more, a fixed penalty notice will not be issued. You will be reported for a summons and are at high risk of disqualification from driving for six months.

Fixed Penalty Notices Affixed to Vehicles

You return to a parked vehicle to find a fixed penalty notice affixed to the windscreen. If you feel aggrieved, there is little point finding the traffic warden or police officer responsible and arguing. The ticket may only be cancelled by the Fixed Penalty Office.

⚠ A MOTORIST parked his vehicle just for a few minutes in a no waiting area and returned to find a traffic warden scribbling away. A heated argument developed and the motorist struck the traffic warden. He was subsequently charged with assault, convicted and sentenced to 28 days' imprisonment. He still had to pay the fixed penalty...

If you feel aggrieved for a good reason you should write to the Fixed Penalty Office stating that reason. The fixed penalty may be cancelled.

You have 28 days in which to pay the fixed penalty. If you do not, the police will send a 'notice to the owner' to the registered keeper of the vehicle:

- giving details of the alleged offence and of the amount of the fixed penalty;

- stating the period allowed for response to the notice;

- indicating that if the fixed penalty is not paid before the end of that period, the registered keeper must provide certain information.

The offence is committed by the person using the vehicle at the date and time of the alleged offence, who may not be the registered keeper. You may have sold the vehicle recently or the vehicle may have been used by someone else with your permission. The effect of this notice to the owner is to protect you in either of those circumstances.

The notice will be sent with two forms: a statutory statement of ownership and a statutory statement of facts. Complete and return the first if you sold the vehicle before the date of the alleged offence. Complete and return the statement of ownership and the statement of facts if a person other than yourself was using the vehicle, giving that person's name and address.

If you do not complete either of these forms you, as the

registered keeper, must pay the fixed penalty. If the offence is endorsable, you will have your licence endorsed. You should be aware, too, that if you provide false information on the forms, you commit an offence that is infinitely more serious than the original fixed penalty offence.

Conditional Offer of a Fixed Penalty

If a police officer believes that a fixed penalty offence has been committed but no fixed penalty notice was affixed to the vehicle or given personally, the police may send a conditional offer of a fixed penalty, together with:

- details of the circumstances of the alleged offence;
- a note of the amount of the fixed penalty;
- a statement to the effect that no further proceedings in respect of that offence will be commenced within 28 days.

Provided the following conditions are fulfilled, no conviction will follow:

- the fixed penalty is paid;
- where the offence is endorsable, the person receiving the notice forwards the driving licence to the Fixed Penalty Office;
- the Fixed Penalty Office clerk is satisfied that the person is not liable for disqualification under the totting-up provisions.

A conditional offer of a fixed penalty may be made when, for example, a police officer has in mind reporting you for a summons but a senior officer advises that the matter may properly be dealt with by way of a fixed penalty.

Administrative Errors

It is not unknown for the Fixed Penalty Office to make an administrative error and claim that you have not paid the penalty when you have. When you pay the fixed penalty, keep the receipt. If you pay by cheque, be sure that you can find the cheque stub.

What Happens if You Do Not Pay a Fixed Penalty?

If a fixed penalty is not paid and you have not completed either of the statutory declarations referred to above, a fine of the fixed penalty plus 50 per cent will be registered against you at a magistrates' court. That fine will be enforced by the court in the same way as other fines. Fail to respond to the fine notice and a warrant for your arrest will almost certainly be issued.

THE POLICE AND ACCIDENTS

If you are the driver of a vehicle involved in an accident in which injury is caused to a person other than yourself, or to a dog or farm animal, or in which damage is caused to another vehicle or to roadside property, you must stop and give your name and address, and the name and address of the owner of the vehicle, and the registration number of the vehicle to anyone having reasonable grounds for requiring them.

You are not obliged to call the police to the scene of an accident. You should be aware that the driver of a vehicle involved in an accident to which the police are called will be required to provide a breath test even if the accident was clearly not the driver's fault.

A MOTORIST who had been out to dinner with his wife drove to within 100 m of his home when his car was in collision with a vehicle driven the wrong way around a roundabout. No one was injured and damage was minimal but the irate motorist insisted on calling the police. Both drivers were required to provide a roadside breath test. He failed, the other driver passed.

He was charged with driving with excess alcohol, convicted, fined £600 and disqualified from driving for 15 months.

Drivers questioned by the police at the scene of an accident, possibly in a state of shock, often say things which they later regret. What you say may amount to an admission of guilt or may destroy your chances of a successful defence to a charge before a court. Four-letter words will be faithfully recorded in the police officer's notebook and are unlikely to impress the magistrates if you subsequently appear in court.

It is a good idea to say as little as possible until you have recovered from the shock and can think clearly. Sit down quietly at the earliest opportunity and make notes of the sequence of events. Sign, date and time the notes. If, at a later date, you are required to give a statement to the police, refer to your notes. If you are charged with an offence and consult a solicitor, take the notes with you.

You are not obliged to report every accident to the police. An extraordinary number of motorists either report an accident unnecessarily or fail to report an accident when they should. This latter could prove to be a very expensive mistake. You are only required to report an accident in the following circumstances:

1. if you did not give your name and address at the time of the accident;

2. if the accident resulted in injury to a person other than yourself and you did not produce your insurance certificate to anyone with reasonable grounds for requesting it.

In such circumstances, you must report the accident in person and as soon as reasonably practicable. The statute includes the words '. . . and in any event, within 24 hours'. Do not be misled into believing that you have 24 hours in which to report an accident.

Summonses and Charges

A SUMMONS

Read the summons and all the accompanying documents carefully.

You are hereby summoned to appear before the magistrates' court sitting at...

This is simply a note of the place, date and time at which your case will first be placed before the court. You are not compelled to attend. The summons continues:

to answer to an information of which particulars appear below.

This is the charge or charges. You should understand that you are not charged, for instance, simply with driving a mechanically propelled vehicle without due care and attention, but with doing so at a particular place, on a particular date and at a given time. Is the charge correct in every detail? Minor errors, like typing mistakes, are of no consequence but substantial errors may form the basis of a defence.

For example, if the date and time of the alleged offence are clearly wrong, you may wish to advise the prosecution

SUMMONS

To: A. N. OTHER
    15 STATION HILL
    MILTOWN
    STAFFORDSHIRE

Date of Information/   7/9/94
        Complaint

| CASE NUMBER | M00000 |

Date of Summons   12/9/94
   Date of Birth   27/11/73

YOU ARE HEREBY SUMMONED TO APPEAR BEFORE THE MAGIS-
TRATES' COURT SITTING AT
MARKET CROSS, MILTOWN, STAFFORDSHIRE
ON 11th DAY OF OCTOBER 1994   AT 10.00 AM
TO ANSWER TO THE INFORMATION   OF WHICH PARTICULARS
ARE GIVEN BELOW

INFORMANT: JOHN PETER BLOGGS, CHIEF SUPERINTENDENT
OF POLICE

1. ON 31/8/94 AT 10.15 AM
   AT LONDON ROAD, MILTOWN, YOU DID DRIVE A
   MOTOR VEHICLE WITHOUT DUE CARE AND ATTENTION
   CONTRARY TO SECTION 3 OF THE ROAD TRAFFIC ACT 1988.

* * * * * * * * * * * * * * * IMPORTANT * * * * * * * * * * * * * * * *
YOU MUST PRODUCE YOUR DRIVING LICENCE AND, IF YOU
HAVE ONE, YOUR COUNTERPART TO THE LICENCE EITHER BY
SENDING THEM TO THE COURT AT LEAST THREE DAYS
BEFORE THE HEARING OR BY HAVING THEM WITH YOU AT
COURT. FAILURE TO PRODUCE YOUR LICENCE MAY RESULT IN
A FINE OF UP TO £400 AND ITS SUSPENSION UNTIL PRODUCED.
* *

Communications relating to this Summons
MUST QUOTE THE CASE NUMBER GIVEN ABOVE
and should be addressed to:
THE CLERK TO THE JUSTICES
JUSTICES' CLERK'S OFFICE

                                        Clerk to the Justices

give them an opportunity to correct their error. On the other hand, you may believe that the prosecution have a duty to get it right without any help from yourself – and plead not guilty.

At the trial a police officer will give evidence of the date and time of the alleged offence. You or your solicitor should cross-examine the officer on this point. Once the wrong details have been confirmed, provided you can show that on that date and at that time you were elsewhere, you should not be convicted.

The prosecution may realise their error and, at any time before the conclusion of their case, make an application to the magistrates to have the charge amended. The magistrates will be advised by the court clerk not to allow any amendment that would destroy your valid defence.

A YOUNG MAN was charged with exceeding the speed limit and pleaded not guilty. Two police officers gave evidence that they had observed his car, registration number *******, driven at a speed of 55 m.p.h. on a road where speed was restricted to 30 m.p.h. Questioned on this point, they each repeated their evidence. When the young man gave evidence that, though the registration number was correct, ******* was the registration number of his *motorcycle*, he was acquitted and awarded costs.

Assuming that you are subsequently found not guilty, the prosecution may substitute a corrected information and you may receive another summons. In summary matters (i.e. charges which may be tried only before a magistrates' court), such an information must be laid within six months of the date of the alleged offence, otherwise it is out of time and cannot proceed further.

In practice, the prosecution will rarely take the trouble to bring the matter to court a second time.

Upon receipt of a summons, whether you intend to plead guilty or not guilty, you may wish to seek an adjournment.

You may wish to take more time to consult a solicitor, or be away on business or on holiday. Telephone the court as soon as possible. Quote the case number and give the reasons why you seek an adjournment. Confirm your telephone call by writing to the clerk to the justices at the address shown on the summons. The court is more likely to grant the adjournment than to refuse it.

The documents accompanying the summons may include the following:

A Statement of Facts

If you intend to plead guilty without attending court, and provided the magistrates deal with your matter there and then, the prosecutor will simply read out the statement of facts. The prosecutor will not be permitted to elaborate further.

Are the facts substantially correct? It you submit a written plea of guilty and, at the same time, dispute the facts, for example if you write:

'I plead guilty to exceeding the speed limit but my speed was nothing like 95 m.p.h., more like 75 m.p.h.'

it is likely that the court will order you to attend so that evidence may be heard from the prosecution, from yourself and any witnesses you may wish to call, in order that the true version of events may be determined.

Notice of Written Plea of Guilty/Notice of Intention to Attend Court

If you decide to plead guilty in absence, you should write to the justices' clerk so that your letter is received at least three days before the date of the hearing. You are entitled to change your mind at any time before the hearing, and may do so either by informing the clerk or by appearing in court

STATEMENT OF FACTS
(MAGISTRATES' COURTS ACT, 1980 s. 12(i)(b))

To: A. N. OTHER
    15 STATION HILL   Case Number   M00000
    MILTOWN
    STAFFORDSHIRE   Date   12/9/94

                             Date of Hearing   11/10/94

COURT MARKET CROSS, MILTOWN, STAFFORDSHIRE

If you inform the Clerk of the Court that you wish to plead guilty to the charge(s) of driving without due care and attention

set out in the Summons(es) served herewith, without appearing before the Court and the Court proceeds to hear and dispose of the case in your absence under section 12 of the Magistrates' Courts Act, 1980 the following statement of facts will be read out in open court before the Court decides whether to accept your plea. If your plea of guilty is accepted the Court will not, unless it adjourns the case after convicting you and before sentencing you, permit any other statement to be made by or on behalf of the Prosecutor with respect to any facts relating to the charge.

STATEMENT OF FACTS

1. ON 31/8/94 AT 10.15 AM
AT LONDON ROAD, MILTOWN

PC JONES, IN THE COMPANY OF PC BROWN, WAS DRIVING AN UNMARKED POLICE CAR ALONG THE A4140 AT MILTOWN IN THE DIRECTION OF STAFFORD. AT THIS TIME HE WAS FOLLOWING A SLOW-MOVING TRACTOR AT A SPEED OF 15 MILES PER HOUR. TRAVELLING BEHIND THEM WAS A PICK-UP TRUCK VEHICLE DRIVEN BY THE DEFENDANT. THE DEFENDANT SUDDENLY PULLED OUT AND COMMENCED TO OVERTAKE BOTH VEHICLES. HE WAS ALONGSIDE THE POLICE VEHICLE WHEN THERE APPEARED AN ONCOMING TRANSIT VAN. THE DEFENDANT CONTINUED TO OVERTAKE. THE VAN WAS FORCED TO BRAKE HARD AND SWERVE INTO ITS NEARSIDE TO AVOID A COLLISION WITH THE DEFENDANT'S VEHICLE. THE DEFENDANT CONTINUED ON PAST THE TRACTOR AND SWERVED BACK INTO THE NEARSIDE IN THE GAP BETWEEN THE TRANSIT AND THE TRACTOR. PC JONES OVERTOOK THE TRACTOR WHEN IT WAS SAFE TO DO SO AND CAUSED THE DEFENDANT TO STOP.
    THE DEFENDANT WAS INTERVIEWED AND SAID 'I MADE A MISTAKE.` HE WAS TOLD THAT THE FACTS WOULD BE REPORTED.

An application will be made for the defendant to pay a contribution towards the costs of the prosecution.

and pleading not guilty. Your written plea of guilty will then be disregarded.

There is a space on the written plea of guilty form for you to write whatever you wish about the offence or about your circumstances. You should take advantage of this. Either write in the space provided or write a letter which will be read to the magistrates before they decide on the appropriate penalty.

A good letter may make a considerable difference to a fine, and if the offence is endorsable and the number of penalty points is variable (e.g. speeding), your letter may persuade the court to impose fewer penalty points. Examples of what you should write (and of what you should very definitely not write) are given in Chapter 10.

The notice of intention to attend court is used when you intend to plead guilty but where you or your solicitor wish to address the court before sentence. You should think very carefully before you adopt this procedure. Except in the circumstances outlined in Chapter 10, it is usually pointless and time-consuming. You should know, too, that if you are present in court, the prosecutor is not restricted to details of the offence contained in the statement of facts and may go into greater detail.

Charged, for example, with driving without due care and attention, the prosecutor is entitled to say that the police officer smelled alcohol on your breath and that you were required to take a roadside breath test. You passed – but there might be an implication that you only just passed.

Notice of Intention to Plead Not Guilty

If you decide to plead not guilty, there is little point in attending court on the date shown on the summons. Your case will not be heard on that date. You or your solicitor should write to the court indicating that you intend to plead not guilty to the charge or one of the charges (make sure you indicate which one).

So that a convenient date may be set aside for the trial, you should list the dates (say within the next eight weeks) when you and any witnesses you may wish to call will be unavailable. So that the court staff will have some idea of how long the trial is likely to take, say how many witnesses you intend to call.

The exception to the above is when you wish to plead not guilty to a charge of having no insurance, no driving licence or no MOT certificate. You may either send the relevant document to the court with a not guilty plea or attend court and produce the document. Provided the prosecution confirms that the document is in order, the charges will be dismissed.

There may, however, also be an alternative charge of failing to produce the document to which, at the same time, you must plead guilty or not guilty (see page 49).

Just as you may change a guilty plea to a not guilty plea at any time before the court hearing, you may change your plea at any time before the court hearing or, indeed, during your trial up until conviction. You should know, however, that if you do change your plea in these circumstances, you will almost certainly have to pay a greater sum in costs and you are likely to find that the court imposes a more severe penalty.

Statement of Means

Since the unit fine system was abolished in September 1993, there is no statutory requirement for courts to include the statement of means form. The majority still do. Some do not.

Most persons convicted of motoring offences are dealt with by way of a fine and the level of the fine will depend on the offence, whether or not it is typical of its type, more serious or less serious, whether or not you have a conviction for a similar offence, and on your means (your ability to pay). Courts are still required to adjust the fine according to your income. While a fine of £100 may mean nothing to a company director earning £40,000 a year, it can spell absolute disaster for a defendant with no income and no savings. So, if you are unemployed or in receipt of a low income, it is absolutely essential that you complete this form. If no such form is included, you should write to the court including details of your income and expenses. If you do neither of these things, you are likely to be fined more than you can afford to pay.

What Will Happen if You Ignore a Summons?

When your matter first comes before a court, it will be adjourned. The summons will be re-dated and served on you again, either by recorded delivery or in person. With the re-dated summons, you will be sent copies of statements – the evidence against you. If you do not attend on the date shown on the summons, provided the court is satisfied that the summons and the evidence were served in time, the magistrates will hear the case in your absence.

The prosecution will prove the matter(s) against you and, if you are convicted of an endorsable offence, your case will again be adjourned and the court will request a print-out of your driving licence from the DVLA. You will be sent either an adjournment notice advising you of the date on which you will be sentenced and requiring you to produce your driving licence, requesting details of your income etc., or you will receive a notice requiring your attendance because the court has disqualification in mind.

If you have been convicted of an offence which is not endorsable, the court may fine you there and then or may send you an adjournment notice together with a request for details of your means.

If you fail to respond to an adjournment notice, you will be sentenced on the date shown. You will be sent a fine notice and, if you were convicted of an endorsable offence, the court may make an order requiring the police to seize your driving licence, and may suspend that licence until it is produced for endorsement.

A CHARGE

For some of the more serious offences, rather than receiving a summons, you are likely to be arrested at the scene of the incident, taken to a police station, charged and cautioned:

You are charged with the offence(s) shown below. You do not have to say anything unless you wish to do so, but what you say may be given in evidence.

Here is an example.

That you on [date] at [place] in the County of [   ] did drive a motor vehicle on the road, having consumed alcohol in such a quantity that the proportion thereof in your breath exceeded the prescribed limit.

Contrary to section 5(1)(a) of the Road Traffic Act, 1988.

There is a space for any reply you make and a space for the date and time charged, and the form will be signed by the arresting officer and the custody officer. Think very carefully before you say anything. If you are to be given bail, you will be given a bail notice and required to read and sign it before you are released:

I understand that my failure to surrender to the magistrates'
court at [place] on [date] at [time] may render me liable to
prosecution under section 6 of the Bail Act, 1976.

Unlike with a summons, you must attend court. If you do
not, a warrant will almost certainly be issued for your arrest
and, in addition to any penalty upon conviction for the original offence, you may be fined or sentenced to a term of
imprisonment for failing to surrender to your bail.

Charged with a motoring offence, the vast majority of
defendants are released on bail. Charged with a serious
offence, e.g. causing death by dangerous driving, you may
be kept in police cells for up to 24 hours, longer if a Sunday
or Bank Holiday intervenes. There are rare circumstances in
which you may be detained for up to 72 hours.

You must ask to see a qualified solicitor. If you do not
know one, ask to see the duty solicitor.

Quite understandably, most persons finding themselves
in this situation are nervous, perhaps in a state of shock, too
garrulous, too truculent or too reticent. It is absolutely
essential that a solicitor is present at any interview. You will
be advised of your rights and of what is likely to happen, and
a member of your family will be contacted.

Bail or Custody?

You will be brought before a court, represented by this same
solicitor. The prosecution may now have no objection to
bail, often with conditions, or may apply to the court for a
further remand in custody. Your solicitor will have discussed
this possibility with you in detail and will answer the prosecutor's application appropriately.

Under the present law, every person has the right to be
released on bail unless it is shown that:

1. the person is likely to commit further offences, if
   released;

2. the person is likely to fail to surrender to bail;

3. the offence is so serious that bail should not be granted;

4. the person is likely to interfere with witnesses, if released;

5. the person has committed the present offence while already on bail;

6. the person has previously failed to surrender to bail;

7. there are any other circumstances which make it preferable to refuse bail.

Although there is a presumption that you should be given bail, there could be a good reason for remanding you in custody.

If the prosecutor applies to the court for a remand in custody, your solicitor may contest that application and apply for bail. Your solicitor will offer the court a settled address, will stress any domestic responsibilities you may have, e.g. a wife and children, and mention the importance of returning to any job you may have as soon as possible. Bail may be refused, or it may be granted with or without conditions. Bail conditions are imposed to ensure (a) that you will answer to that bail (i.e. turn up on the date of the hearing) and (b) that you commit no further offences in the meantime. Conditions may include:

● residence at a particular address, usually your home address;

● reporting to your nearest police station at a given time on particular days of the week;

● a requirement that you do not enter licensed premises;

● a requirement that you do not associate with a particular person or persons.

Treat Bail Conditions with the Utmost Respect

Break a condition of bail and you are likely to be arrested and, when you appear before a court again, your chances of being given bail a second time will not be good. If bail is refused you will be conveyed to a remand prison. Your solicitor may make an application for bail to a judge in chambers. If that too fails, you will remain in custody and will be brought before the magistrates' court again after seven or eight days. A further remand in custody may be for up to 28 days.

You should know that your solicitor may make only one further application for bail before a magistrates' court. Subsequent applications may only be made if there is a change in circumstances. Your solicitor will advise you what may constitute such a change.

When your matter comes to court, if you are convicted and sentenced to a term of imprisonment, any period spent in custody before conviction will be deducted from the total sentence. If you are acquitted, all the time you have spent in custody counts for nothing – you have been imprisoned for a crime you did not commit. In 1991, statistics show that 17 per cent of prisoners remanded before conviction were subsequently found not guilty.

PART II

The Offences

Offences and
Likely Penalties

Offences which may only be dealt with by way of a fixed penalty or by a magistrates' court are known as summary offences. Offences which may be dealt with by either a magistrates' court or a Crown Court are **either way** offences, and those that may only be dealt with by a Crown Court are known as indictable offences.

There are over 1000 motoring offences but some 40 or 50 of these account for 99 per cent of the work of the courts. We deal only with these common offences and on the following pages indicate whether or not a **fixed penalty** is available, and whether or not a **Vehicle Defect Rectification Scheme Notice** may be issued (see Chapter 1).

We will also look at the likely penalty upon conviction and you will see at a glance whether or not the offence is **endorsable** (and the number of penalty points applicable).

Key Terms

■ **Either way offence** An offence which may be tried either by a magistrates' court or before a judge and jury at a Crown Court ■ **Fixed penalty** Provides an opportunity to have the matter dealt with other than by a court ■ **VDRS** A scheme whereby a motorist is given an opportunity to put right vehicle defects without penalty ■ **Endorsement** The annotation of your driving licence with penalty points

We list those offences for which disqualification from driving is compulsory upon conviction, and those offences for which disqualification upon conviction is a very real possibility.

LIKELY PENALTY

The vast majority of motoring offenders are dealt with by way of a fine and the level of fine is set by statute, reflecting the seriousness with which the offence is regarded. Thus, failing to wear a seatbelt is a Level 2 offence. Using a vehicle without a test certificate is a Level 3 offence. Driving with excess alcohol is a Level 5 offence.

The level of fine for each of the most common offences is listed in Chapters 4 to 8.

The maximum fine that a court may impose upon conviction depends on the level attributed to the particular offence:

Maximum Fines (1994)	
Level 1	£200
Level 2	£500
Level 3	£1000
Level 4	£2500
Level 5	£5000

While courts have been known to impose such maximum fines, magistrates and judges would have to regard the offence as very serious indeed to even approach such levels. In fact, usually, the fine imposed is no more than a fraction of the above.

To illustrate this point, the following were taken at random from newspaper reports published in July 1994.

A motorist who drove at 124 m.p.h on a motorway was fined £300, licence endorsed with 6 penalty points and disqualified from driving for four months.

For driving without due care and attention, a motorist who was unemployed was fined £60, licence endorsed with 6 penalty points.

For failing to produce his driving licence and test certificate, a motorist was fined £30 on each charge.

For driving without insurance, an unemployed motorist was fined £120, licence endorsed with 8 penalty points and disqualified from driving for 28 days.

A motorist was fined £60 for driving not in accordance with a licence.

Every case is different and the fine imposed will depend on:

● the circumstances of the offence, i.e. whether or not the facts reveal a pretty typical example of the offence, whether the court regards the offence as less serious or more serious than a typical example;

● whether or not the defendant has a previous conviction or convictions for an offence of a similar nature;

● the means of the defendant, the defendant's ability to pay, whether or not the defendant is unemployed or in receipt of a low income.

It is also true to say that a defendant who pleads guilty and is fined may well have to pay a smaller fine than a defendant who is charged with the same offence in exactly the same circumstances who pleads not guilty but after a trial is found guilty.

PENALTIES OTHER THAN A FINE

There is no doubt that the two penalties most feared by motoring offenders are (a) a term of imprisonment and (b) disqualification from driving.

Likelihood of Imprisonment

The only common offences for which, upon conviction, a term of imprisonment is possible are as follows:

Summary offences

accident, failing to stop and failing to report;

driving with excess alcohol;

after driving, refusing to provide specimens for analysis;

being in charge with excess alcohol;

after being in charge, refusing to provide specimens for analysis;

driving while disqualified;

taking a vehicle without consent.

Either way offences

aggravated vehicle taking;

causing danger to road users;

dangerous driving.

Indictable offences

causing death by careless driving while under the influence of drink or drugs;

causing death by dangerous driving;

manslaughter, involving a motor vehicle.

Of the summary offences, you are at greatest risk of a term of imprisonment if you drive while disqualified. The risk of a term of imprisonment is high if you are convicted of one of the either way offences and a term of imprisonment is almost inevitable upon conviction for one of the indictable offences.

Likelihood of Disqualification

Disqualification from driving is, in theory at least, a sentence which may be imposed for any endorsable offence. There are, however, offences for which, upon conviction, disqualification is compulsory and there are offences for which, upon conviction, the risk of disqualification is high.

Offences for which disqualification from driving is compulsory are:

causing death by careless driving while under the influence etc.;

causing death by dangerous driving;

manslaughter, involving a motor vehicle;

aggravated vehicle taking;

dangerous driving;

driving with excess alcohol;

after driving, refusing to provide specimens for analysis.

TABLE OF OFFENCES

Offence	Is it a fixed penalty offence?	What penalty is a court likely to impose?	Is the offence endorsable?	Is disqualification likely?	Page number in this book
Summary offences not endorsable					
Carried, allowing yourself to be carried in a vehicle etc.	No	Fine/imprisonment	No	N/A	60
Documents, failing to produce	No	Fine	No	N/A	49
No vehicle excise licence	No	Fine plus back duty	No	N/A	51
Exhaust emission offences	Yes, VDRS possible	Fine	No	N/A	55
Helmet, no safety	Yes	Fine	No	N/A	55
Lighting offences	Yes, VDRS possible	Fine	No	N/A	55
Ownership, not notifying change	Yes	Fine	No	N/A	55
Ownership/driver, failing to supply details of	Yes	Fine	No	N/A	56
Most parking offences	Yes	Fine	No	N/A	55
Seatbelt offences	Yes	Fine	No	N/A	55
Taking a vehicle without consent	No	Community penalty	No	Yes	58
Test certificate, no	No	Fine	No	N/A	62
Summary offences endorsable					
Accident, failing to stop	No	Fine	5–10	Yes	64
Accident, failing to report	No	Fine	5–10	Yes	67
Defective tyre	Yes, VDRS possible	Fine	3	No	70
Double white lines, failing to comply	No	Fine	3	No	70
Driving without due care	No	Fine	3–11	Only in the most serious cases	73
Driving while disqualified	No	Imprisonment/community penalty	6	Yes, for a further period	79
Driving not in accordance with a licence	Yes	Fine	3–6	Yes, for unsupervised learner	77
Insurance, using a vehicle without	No	Fine	6–8	Yes, especially if deliberate	83
Leaving in dangerous position	Yes	Fine	3	No	89
Load, insecure	No	Fine	3	No	90
Pedestrian crossing offences	Yes	Fine	3	School crossing, in serious cases	92

Offence	Fixed penalty	Penalty	Points	Disqualification	Page
Speeding, exceeding speed limit	Yes	Fine	3–6	Yes, especially if 30 m.p.h. or more above limit	99
Traffic lights, failing to comply with	Yes	Fine	3	No	105
Police/traffic signs, failing to comply with	Yes	Fine	3	No	105
Using a vehicle in a dangerous condition	Yes, VDRS possible	Fine	3	No	105
Motorway offences					
Exceeding 70 m.p.h.	Yes	Fine	3–6	Yes, at 100 m.p.h. or more	107
Exceeding contraflow speed limit	Yes	Fine	3	Yes, at high speeds	109
Stopping on hard shoulder	Yes	Fine	No	N/A	110
Driving in contravention of traffic sign	Yes	Fine	3	No	117
Driving on hard shoulder	Yes	Fine	3	No	112
Driving in reverse	Yes	Fine	3	No	113
Driving in wrong direction	Yes, but unlikely	Fine	3	Yes	113
Learner driver on motorway	Yes	Fine	3	No	114
Making U-turn	Yes, but unlikely	Fine	3	Yes	115
Unauthorised vehicle in third lane	Yes	Fine	3	No	116
Alcohol-related offences					
Refusing roadside breath test	No	Fine	4	No	125
In charge, with excess alcohol	No	Fine	10	Yes	132
After being in charge, refusing to provide specimens for analysis	No	Fine	10	Yes	136
Driving with excess alcohol	No	Fine	(4)	Compulsory	128
After driving, refusing to provide specimens for analysis	No	Fine	(4)	Compulsory	134
Either way offences before a magistrates' court					
Aggravated vehicle taking	No	Imprisonment	(4)	Compulsory	148
Causing danger to road users	No	Imprisonment	No	N/A	152
Dangerous driving	No	Community penalty/imprisonment	(6)	Compulsory, compulsory re-test	153
Fraudulent use of excise licence	No	Fine	No	N/A	158

There is a real risk of disqualification upon conviction for one of the following offences:

accident, failing to stop/failing to report;

driving without insurance;

taking a vehicle without consent;

driving in the wrong direction on a motorway;

making a U-turn on a motorway;

being in charge of a motor vehicle with excess alcohol;

after being in charge, refusing to provide specimens for analysis.

And, in the following circumstances:

upon conviction for exceeding the speed limit when the facts reveal that the speed was 30 m.p.h or more above the legal limit;

under the 'totting-up' provisions (see Chapter 10).

In Chapters 4 to 8, the offences are examined in some detail. First, the statute is quoted and the constituent elements of the offence are explained. The question is asked, what must the prosecution prove if you are to be convicted of the offence? Possible defences are given, together with advice as to what to do (and what not to do) if charged with the offence. Maximum penalties upon conviction are shown. Specific defences to each charge are outlined. There is a defence which is common to all motoring charges, indeed to charges of any nature, and that is a defence based on identification: 'It wasn't me, I wasn't there.'

Summary Offences Which Are Not Endorsable

DOCUMENTS, FAILING TO PRODUCE

On [date] at [place] being the driver of a motor vehicle/being a person whom a police constable had reasonable cause to believe to have been the driver of a motor vehicle at a time when an accident occurred owing to its presence on [road]/being a person a police constable had reasonable cause to believe to have committed an offence . . . on being so required by a police constable, did fail to produce for examination the relevant certificate of insurance/test certificate/driving licence.

Contrary to section 165(1) of the Road Traffic Act, 1988.

Maximum Penalty

Level 2 fine.

The document must be produced at the police station nominated by you within the time specified. You are not required to produce the document personally; someone else may produce it for you. The person producing the document must remain at the police station long enough to allow the police to examine the document and make a note of its production in the Police Enquiries Book. The original must be produced. A photocopy or a fax is not acceptable.

Defence

It was not reasonably practicable to produce the document before the summons was issued but the document was produced immediately it became available.

It is not reasonably practicable to produce a driving licence which has been sent to the DVLA. It may not be reasonably practicable to produce an insurance certificate for a company car.

What You Should Do

If you keep your driving licence, insurance certificate and MOT certificate with you at all times, you cannot commit this offence.

If you or your representative are unable to produce the document within the time specified, attend the police station and request further time. If the police station that you nominated is closed, produce the document at another police station. Inform the nominated police station that you produced the document at the other named police station. Always make a note of the date and time the police station was attended, and, if possible, the number of the police officer or the name of the person dealing with the matter.

If, despite the above, you receive a summons and decide to plead quilty, it is worth writing a letter explaining why you failed to produce the document. The court may impose a smaller fine. If your reason is good enough, you may even be granted an absolute discharge.

NO EXCISE LICENCE

*On [date] at [place] you used/kept on a public road namely
. . . a mechanically propelled vehicle namely . . . for which a
licence under the Vehicles (Excise) Act 1971 was not in force.*

Contrary to section 8(1) of the Vehicles (Excise) Act, 1971.

Maximum Penalty

Level 3 fine or five times duty payable 'whichever is the
greater' plus, where the defendant is the keeper, any
unpaid back duty.

The offence is committed by the person using the vehicle,
not necessarily the person driving the vehicle. The person
using the vehicle may not be the owner or keeper of the vehicle, but may, for example, simply have borrowed the vehicle
or be using the vehicle in the course of employment.

Whether the vehicle is yours or not, if you use it and it
has no excise (tax), that becomes your responsibility.

A YOUNG WOMAN borrowed her boyfriend's
car and was stopped by the police. The police officer observed that the excise licence had expired
two months previously. A summons was issued alleging that
she had used a vehicle without an excise licence. She
attended court and pleaded not guilty because it wasn't her
car. She was convicted, fined £60 and ordered to pay the
costs of the prosecution.

The offence is committed when an untaxed vehicle is on a
public road. The vehicle does not have to be a motor vehicle
but any mechanically propelled vehicle, e.g. a vehicle propelled by electricity, steam etc.

Exempted Vehicles

Exempted vehicles are snow ploughs, and vehicles used by HM forces or Crown employees in certain stipulated circumstances. Trade licence plate holders testing or delivering vehicles are also exempted.

A special exemption licence is granted to vehicles used solely for the purpose of carrying a disabled person and vehicles (e.g. an agricultural tractor using a public road to pass from field to field) which are not driven on the road for a distance greater than six miles in any week.

Defences

1. You were not the person using the vehicle.

2. The vehicle is not a mechanically propelled vehicle.

3. The vehicle has a special exemption licence.

4. The vehicle was not used on a public road.

5. You were driving the vehicle to an MOT centre for a pre-booked MOT.

A YOUNG MAN was observed by the police driving a Ford Escort which had no tax disc displayed in the windscreen. Asked for an explanation, he said that he was taking it for an MOT. He gave the name of the garage to which he was taking the vehicle. Enquiries were made and revealed that the vehicle had not been booked in for an MOT. A summons was issued alleging that the vehicle had been used without an excise licence.

The young man pleaded guilty in absence, was fined £120 and ordered to pay £30 towards the costs of the prosecution.

Back Duty

The registered keeper of a vehicle who is convicted of this offence is liable for the payment of any back duty owed.

Defences to a claim for back duty

1. You were not the registered keeper of the vehicle for the period alleged.
2. You have already paid some or all of the back duty claimed.

A MOTORIST was charged with using a vehicle without an excise licence and the DVLA made a claim for £180 in back duty. The motorist pleaded guilty to the offence but disputed the back duty, saying that he had only bought the car the week before. He was unable to produce any documentation to prove this, neither could he remember the name of the person from whom he had bought the vehicle.

He was fined £300, ordered to pay prosecution costs and to pay the back duty in full.

It is not a defence to a claim for back duty that the vehicle was off the road for part of the time for which back duty is claimed.

A MOTORIST bought an MGB and became the registered keeper on 28 October 1993. The tax for the vehicle expired on 30 November 1993, but he spent the winter restoring the vehicle and did not use it on a public road until 4 April 1994. The vehicle was observed parked on the road with an out of date tax disc and a summons was issued. The DVLA made a claim for back duty from 1 December 1993.

The motorist attended court and pleaded guilty to the offence of using a vehicle on the road without an excise licence but disputed the claim for back duty. He was fined £60 and ordered to pay the back duty in full.

A VEHICLE FAILED its MOT and the registered keeper, who was unemployed, could not afford to pay for the necessary repairs. Not having a garage, he left the car parked on the road outside his house intending to carry out the work himself. The tax ran out. The vehicle was observed by the police and a summons was issued. The DVLA claimed back duty from the date that the tax expired.

The motorist attended court and pleaded not guilty to the offence. The basis of his defence was that the car could not be driven and had not been driven without an excise licence. He was convicted of the offence, fined £50 and ordered to pay the costs of the prosecution. He was ordered to pay the back duty in full.

Mitigated Penalties

Motorists who do not renew their excise licence may receive a notice advising them of this and giving them an opportunity to pay the back duty owed, plus a small sum to cover the cost of administration. Those who fail to take advantage of this 'mitigated penalty' are likely to receive a summons alleging that they used a vehicle without an excise licence.

A motorist who receives a summons in these circumstances, and who either pleads guilty or is found guilty, will find that the total of the fine imposed and the prosecution costs will be much greater than the mitigated penalty.

What you should do

If you intend to plead guilty to the charge and there is no claim for back duty, plead guilty in absence. If you intend to plead not guilty, be very sure that you have a defence to the charge. On the day of the hearing see the duty solicitor, who will advise you whether or not you have a defence and advise you how best to present your case.

Do not plead not guilty simply because you believe that the DVLA are demanding far too much in back duty. Attend court and plead guilty to the offence, and then explain to the magistrates why you believe that the claim for back duty is wrong.

- **EXHAUST EMISSION OFFENCES**
- **HELMET, NO SAFETY**
- **LIGHTING OFFENCES**
- **OWNERSHIP, FAILING TO NOTIFY CHANGE**
- **MOST PARKING OFFENCES**
- **SEATBELT OFFENCES**

These are all offences which are not endorsable and for which the **fixed penalty** procedure is available. A **VDRS notice** may be issued for exhaust emission offences and for lighting offences. Take advantage of either of these options. Do not attend court unless you are confident that you have a defence to the charge.

Key Terms

Fixed penalty Provides an opportunity to have the matter dealt with other than by a court ■ **VDRS** A scheme whereby a motorist is given an opportunity to put right vehicle defects without penalty

OWNERSHIP/DRIVER, FAILING TO SUPPLY DETAILS OF

1.   On [date] at [place] you did fail, upon being required by or on behalf of the Chief Officer of Police for . . . to give information which it was in your power to give and which may have led to the identification of the driver of a motor vehicle, registration number ... alleged to have been guilty of an offence under section 14 of the Road Traffic Regulation Act 1984 on the M[   ] Motorway on [date].

Contrary to section 112(4) of the Road Traffic Regulation Act, 1984.

2.   On [date] at [place] having been required on behalf of the Chief Officer of Police for ... to give such information as was in your power to give and which might have led to the identification of the driver of a certain motor vehicle . . ./rider of a certain cycle . . . who was alleged to be guilty of an offence under . . . did fail to do so.

Contrary to section 172(2) of the Road Traffic Act, 1988.

3.   On [date] at [place] having been required on behalf of the Chief Officer of Police for . . . to give such information as was in your power to give and which might lead to the identification of the driver of a certain vehicle namely [type] registration number . . . at [place] on [date] who was alleged to be guilty of an offence under . . . did fail to do so.

Contrary to section 172 of the Road Traffic Act, 1988.

Maximum Penalty

Level 3 fine.

Fixed penalty available.

Guilty in absence procedure applies.

The registered keeper of a vehicle may receive a notice from the police requiring the keeper to provide information as to who was driving the vehicle on a particular date at a particular place. The notice is most commonly served in the following circumstances.

Speeding Offences Recorded on Camera

The camera photographs the registration plate of the vehicle. A computer records that number, the type and make of the vehicle, the time, date and place, and the speed recorded.

Speeding Offences in a Motorway Contraflow System

The same procedure is followed and the same details recorded in circumstances where it is clearly unsafe to stop the vehicle.

Offences Where The Driver Is Not Present or When It Was Not Possible to Stop the Vehicle

The registered keeper of the vehicle may be required to give details of the driver who, for example, commits a parking offence or who is observed committing a traffic offence in circumstances where it is not possible to stop the vehicle.

Defences

The offence is committed if you fail to respond to the notice. It is an absolute offence: either you replied or you did not.

You may not know who was driving, or you may have sold the vehicle, but you must still respond to the notice.

TAKING A VEHICLE WITHOUT CONSENT

On [date] at [place] without having the consent of the owner or other lawful authority you took a conveyance, namely . . . for your own or another's use.

Contrary to section 12 of the Theft Act, 1968.

Maximum Penalty

Level 5 fine and/or six months' imprisonment.

Disqualification from driving at the court's discretion.

No fixed penalty available.

No facility to plead guilty in absence.

In practice, the court will take a serious view when the offence is planned, when a vehicle is broken into and 'hot wired' (ignition fired without using an engine key), where a number of persons are involved or when the offence is committed while on bail. If the offence was committed as a result of a misunderstanding with the owner, the court will take a less serious view.

The offence is not endorsable but disqualification from driving is possible. Compensation may be ordered.

The conveyance may be anything from an aircraft to a rowing boat. For the purposes of this book, however, a conveyance is a mechanically propelled vehicle intended or adapted for road use.

It is necessary for the prosecution to prove the following elements:

1. that you did not have the consent of the owner or other lawful authority;

2. that you took the vehicle for your own or another's use.

The 'Consent of the Owner'

The consent of the owner may be implied but it is not consent if it has been obtained by intimidation. A vehicle is taken without consent if the owner gives permission for it to be used for a specific purpose and it is used for a different purpose.

For example, a building worker had his employer's consent to use a van during the course of his employment, and to use it for the purpose of travelling to and from work. When, however, he used it to visit his girlfriend who lived 10 miles from his home, he was reported and charged with taking the vehicle without consent.

'Lawful Authority'

A person who, for example, is ordered to move a vehicle in an emergency, even without the consent of the owner, does so with lawful authority. You may, for example, move a vehicle in order to clear the way for an ambulance or fire engine.

'Taking'

Taking a conveyance constitutes the offence: it is not a necessary element of the offence that you drove it away.

'For Your Use or That of Another'

The word 'use' here means use as a form of transport.

Defences

1. Mistaken identity. You were not the person who took the vehicle.

2. The vehicle was not taken.

3. You had the consent of the owner or lawful authority. Consent obtained by false pretences may still constitute consent. For example, you ask a friend if you may borrow his car 'just to drive into Leeds and back'. He gives his consent, you borrow his car but, in fact, you had no intention simply to drive into Leeds and back; you intended to drive to York. Effectively, you obtained the consent of the owner by false pretences, but you would still have a defence to a charge of taking without consent.

4. You had a valid belief that, if the owner of the vehicle had known of the circumstances, he would have given his consent. The fact that you committed another offence, e.g. driving with excess alcohol, does not invalidate this defence. You will have to give evidence and call witnesses in support of your belief. It is then up to the prosecution to disprove it.

ALLOWING YOURSELF TO BE CARRIED IN A VEHICLE TAKEN WITHOUT CONSENT

On [date] at [place] knowing that a conveyance, namely . . . had been taken without the consent of the owner or other lawful authority, you drove it/allowed yourself to be carried in or on it.

Contrary to section 12 of the Theft Act, 1968.

Maximum Penalty

Level 5 fine and/or six months' imprisonment.

A person allowing himself to be carried is unlikely to be disqualified from driving.

No fixed penalty.

No facility to plead guilty in absence.

The prosecution must prove:

1. that you allowed yourself to be carried in or on the vehicle;

2. that you did so knowing that the vehicle had been taken unlawfully;

3. that the vehicle was driven, i.e. it was in motion.

Defences

1. Mistaken identity: you were not the person carried in or on the vehicle.

2. You were carried in or on the vehicle but you did not know that the vehicle had been taken unlawfully.

3. You were not in or on the vehicle when it was in motion.

There is no such charge as attempting to commit either of the above offences, but a person may be charged with aiding and abetting. The penalties are the same.

What You Should Do

Charged with one of the above offences, consult a solicitor or see the duty solicitor on the date of your court appearance.

USING A VEHICLE WITHOUT A TEST CERTIFICATE

On [date] at [place] you used/caused to be used/permitted to be used on a road a motor vehicle as respects which no test certificate had been issued within the appropriate period.

Contrary to section 47 of the Road Traffic Act, 1988, as amended by the Road Traffic (Consequential Provisions) Act, 1988, Schedule 2.

Maximum Penalty

Level 3 fine.

Level 4 fine where the vehicle is adapted to carry more than eight passengers.

No fixed penalty available.

The requirement for a test certificate applies to vehicles over three years old, excepting those registered before the Road Traffic Act, 1920 came into force. The 'appropriate period' quoted in the statute is 12 months.

The person using the vehicle is the person responsible for the test certificate, so if you borrow a friend's car which should have a test certificate but it does not, you are the person to whom any summons will be addressed. The registered keeper of the vehicle may be summoned for causing or permitting the use of a vehicle without a test certificate.

Defences

1. The vehicle was not more than three years old.

2. The vehicle was not used on a road.

3. The vehicle was not a motor vehicle.

4. At the date of the alleged offence you had a valid test certificate.

What You Should Do

If you intend to plead guilty, there is no need to attend court; you should plead guilty in absence. If you intend to plead not guilty and you have a test certificate which was valid at the date of the alleged offence, simply send it to the court together with your not guilty plea. Provided the prosecution find the document in order, you will not be convicted.

Often, motorists who receive a summons alleging this offence will also be charged with failing to produce a test certificate. This is an alternative charge. You cannot produce what you do not have. You may be guilty of one charge but you cannot be convicted of both. (See 'Documents, Failing to Produce' on page 49.)

If you are unable to find the relevant test certificate but have reason to believe that, given time, you will be able to find it, write to or telephone the court requesting an adjournment.

Summary Offences Which Are Endorsable

FAILING TO STOP/GIVE PARTICULARS AFTER ACCIDENT

On [date] at [place] being the driver of a mechanically propelled vehicle, namely [type of vehicle] owing to the presence of which on a road, namely [name of road] an accident occurred whereby personal injury/damage [either one or both] was caused to another person/another vehicle/an animal not in or on that vehicle or a trailer drawn by that vehicle/property forming part of the land on which the road was situated or land adjacent thereto [one or more of these may apply] failed to stop/and on being required by a person to give your name and address and the name and address of the owner and the identification mark of the vehicle, failed to do so.

Contrary to section 170(4) of the Road Traffic Act, 1988 and Schedule 2 of the Road Traffic Offenders Act, 1988.

Maximum Penalty

Six months' imprisonment and/or a fine not exceeding Level 5.

Endorsement with 5–10 penalty points, disqualification discretionary.

Endorsement codes

Failing to stop: Endorsement Code AC10.

Failing to give particulars: Endorsement Code AC20.

Fixed penalty not available.

Guilty plea in absence not available.

There is a risk of disqualification from driving, particularly if you fail to stop and fail to report the accident. The Road Traffic Act, 1991 introduced imprisonment upon conviction for these offences. The court will take a serious view in the following circumstances:

1. where failure to stop represents an attempt to evade the consequences of being required to provide a breath test;

2. failing to stop/remain at the scene when serious injury is caused.

The offence may be committed only by the driver. If you were not driving, you cannot commit the offence.

The vehicle need not necessarily be a motor vehicle, such as a car, van, lorry etc. The offence may be committed by the driver of any mechanically propelled vehicle (e.g. a dumper truck), whether or not such a vehicle is intended or adapted for road use. Certain pedestrian-controlled vehicles (e.g. grass-cutting machines) are, however, excluded. A trailer is defined as a vehicle drawn by a motor vehicle.

The offence may only be committed on a road, a highway or any other road to which the public have access,

---

Key Terms

■ **Endorsement codes** A code which appears against an endorsement on a driving licence to identify the offences committed

including bridges over which a road passes. Footpaths and bridleways are excluded.

Having been on a road, the vehicle must have been involved in an accident; there must have been a direct cause or connection between the vehicle and the occurrence of the accident.

The offence is committed only where the accident results in injury or damage as in one of the four elements described in the wording of the offence. Note that if you, the driver, are injured and/or your vehicle damaged, but there are no other injuries or damage, you are not obliged to stop. You should be aware, however, that damage to property includes damage to, for instance, road signs, lamp standards, the road itself, even hedgerows, so it is difficult to envisage circumstances where you are injured and/or your vehicle damaged when there is no damage to anything else.

The obligation to stop arises immediately the accident occurs and you must personally remain where you have stopped for as long as is necessary to give the information required, i.e. your name and address, the name and address of the owner of the vehicle, and the registration number. You are not obliged to go and seek out persons who may have a right to such information.

If you have given the above details at the scene of the accident, you do not have to report the accident to the police.

Defences

The prosecution must prove beyond a reasonable doubt that an accident occurred, that you as the driver had a statutory duty to stop and that you failed to do so.

It is a defence if you satisfy the court that you were unaware that an accident had occurred. For example, you may say that the collision was so slight that there was no noise or movement, you felt no bump, you observed no damage to your vehicle.

It could be a defence that the damage may have been there before or that only part of the damage was caused by the accident.

FAILING TO REPORT AN ACCIDENT

On [date] at [place] being the driver of a mechanically propelled vehicle, namely [type of vehicle], owing to the presence of which on a road, namely [name of road], an accident occurred whereby personal injury [one or both] was caused to [another person/another vehicle/an animal not in or on that vehicle or a trailer drawn by that vehicle/property forming part of the land on which the road is situated or land adjacent thereto] and, not having given your name and address to a person having reasonable grounds for requiring you to do so, failed to report the accident at a police station or to a constable as soon as reasonably practicable and in any case within 24 hours of the occurrence of the accident.

Contrary to section 170(4) of the Road Traffic Act, 1988 and Schedule 2 of the Road Traffic Offenders Act, 1988.

Maximum Penalty

Six months' imprisonment and/or a fine not exceeding Level 5.

Endorsement with 5–10 penalty points.

Endorsement Code AC10.

Disqualification discretionary.

Fixed penalty not available.

Guilty plea in absence not available.

The court will regard the offence as serious in the following circumstances:

1. where failure to stop represents an attempt to evade the consequences of being required to provide a breath test;

2. failing to stop/remain at the scene when serious injury is caused.

The obligation to report an accident extends to every case where you have not given your name and address etc. at the scene of the accident. There may, for instance, have been no one present at the scene if the accident occurred in the early hours of the morning.

You must report the accident personally to a police officer, clearly identifying the accident, giving the date, time and place, your name and address, the name and address of the owner of the vehicle, and the registration number.

Do not be misled by the words 'within 24 hours'. You are required to report the accident as soon as reasonably practicable and only then within 24 hours.

Defences

Again it is a defence that you were unaware of any accident. If, however, you become aware within 24 hours of the incident that you have been involved in an accident (if, for example, you observe damage to your vehicle, and put two and two together), you must still report the accident.

If, as a result of the accident, you were taken to hospital and are unable to report the accident within 24 hours because of your incapacity throughout that time, this will be a defence.

What You Should Do

If you intend to plead guilty to either charge, you cannot do so in absence. You will have to attend court and explain why you failed to stop or failed to report.

If you are charged with both offences, if there is evidence that you had been drinking or if you failed to stop after being involved in an accident in which injury was caused, you should consult a solicitor or see the duty solicitor on the day of your court appearance.

Under no circumstances should you plead guilty if you were genuinely unaware that an accident had occurred.

A SCHOOL BUS reversed into a parked car. The children called out a warning to the driver but they were always shouting and screaming anyway and, in order to concentrate on his driving, he had learned to ignore them. He drove off and a passer-by telephoned the police. Stopped ten minutes later, the bus driver was charged with driving without due care and attention, and with failing to stop after an accident. He attended court and pleaded guilty to both charges.

Asked what he wished to say, he apologised to the court and said he did not realise he had been involved in an accident. The clerk advised the magistrates that they should not accept the guilty plea in respect of the second charge. The matters were adjourned to allow the defendant to see the duty solicitor. Having taken advice, he pleaded guilty to careless driving but not guilty to failing to stop. The prosecution accepted his explanation and the failing to stop charge was withdrawn.

AT 11.30 ONE EVENING, a vehicle collided with the rear of another one, reversed and drove off at speed. The incident was observed by a police officer in a patrol car who gave chase and caused the vehicle to stop. The driver was found to be a young man who was on bail awaiting a court appearance for burglary. The conditions of his bail included a curfew between the hours of 8.00 p.m. and 8.00 a.m.

The young man was brought before a court and remanded in custody until the burglary matter was dealt with. In addition to that matter, he was charged with failing to stop. He pleaded guilty to both charges, was sentenced to two consecutive terms of community service and disqualified from driving for six months.

DEFECTIVE TYRE

If a **VDRS notice** is issued, comply with it or take advantage of the offer of a **fixed penalty**. If you receive a summons and intend to plead guilty, do so in absence.

DOUBLE WHITE LINES

Stopping on Double White Lines

On [date] at [place] being the person driving a motor vehicle on a road you did fail to conform with the indication given by a traffic sign, namely double white line markings, in that the vehicle did stop at a point between the two ends of the marking.

Contrary to section 36, Road Traffic Act, 1988.

Key Terms

■ **VDRS** A scheme whereby a motorist is given an opportunity to put right vehicle defects without penalty ■ **Fixed penalty** Provides an opportunity to have the matter dealt with other than by a court

Contravention of Double White Lines

On [date] at [place] being the person driving a motor vehicle on a road you did fail to conform with the indication given by a traffic sign, namely double white line markings, in that where a continuous line was on the left of the other line, the vehicle was not driven so as to keep the continuous line to the right hand or offside of the vehicle.

Contrary to section 36, Road Traffic Act, 1988.

Maximum Penalty

Level 3 fine.

Licence endorsed with 3 penalty points

Endorsement Code TS20.

Disqualification at the discretion of the court.

Fixed penalty available.

Guilty plea in absence procedure available.

A double white line system consists of one of the following:

- two continuous white lines;
- two continuous white lines with hatching between them;
- one continuous white line and one broken white line.

The lines must be painted white and comply with the regulations. A warning arrow must be painted on the road.
    You commit an offence if you:

- stop on either side of a road within such a system; or
- drive on the wrong side of a double white line system, even though it is perfectly safe to do so.

You must either be told that you will be reported for this offence or be sent a written notice of intended prosecution before you are summoned.

Defences

You stopped within a double white line system in circumstances beyond your control, e.g. a breakdown.
    You crossed a continuous white line:

1. in order to gain access to a side road, adjoining land or premises;

2. in order to pass a stationary (not a slow-moving) vehicle;

3. in order to avoid an accident;

4. under the direction of a police officer in uniform;

5. in circumstances beyond your control.

A motorist who overtakes a vehicle immediately before a double white line system and then finds that he or she has to drive on the wrong side of the system for some distance before safely returning to the left-hand side of the road cannot claim that the circumstances were beyond the motorist's control.

What You Should Do

If you committed the offence, either pay the fixed penalty or, if you receive a summons, plead guilty in absence. Do not attend court.

CARELESS AND INCONSIDERATE DRIVING

On [date] at [place] you drove a motor vehicle on a road namely [   ] without due care and attention.

[   ] you drove a motor vehicle on a road namely [   ] without reasonable consideration for other persons using the road.

Contrary to section 3 of the Road Traffic Act, 1988.

These are offences which require a warning or notice of intended prosecution to be given before you are charged. Careless driving and inconsiderate driving are two separate offences, and an information charging you with one OR the other offence is unfair and materially wrong.

Maximum Penalty

Level 4 fine.

Licence endorsed with between 3 and 9 penalty points.

Endorsement Code CD10 (careless); CD20 (inconsiderate).

Disqualification from driving at the discretion of the court.

Compensation may be ordered.

No fixed penalty available.

Facility to plead guilty in absence available.

Driving Without Due Care and Attention

The most likely penalty is a fine and endorsement with whatever number of penalty points the court believes appropriate. Poor weather conditions, a bad road surface, restricted visibility, negligible damage etc. are all factors which the court may take into consideration in deciding on the number of penalty points.

Disqualification from driving is a possibility in cases where the carelessness creates a serious risk of injury or serious damage, or where excessive speed is a factor. A previous conviction for a similar offence may increase the risk of disqualification.

When sentencing, the magistrates are required to consider the cause, not the effect. Thus the fact that someone has been seriously injured or even killed as a result of your driving is not relevant. What is relevant is how far you departed from the standard of driving that would be exercised by a reasonable, prudent, competent driver in all the circumstances of your case.

This principle of cause rather than effect is not well understood by the public, nor, it seems, by members of the press. It is understandable that the relatives of a person killed as a result of careless driving should be angry when the sentence of the court is no more than a fine of £200 and licence endorsed with 6 penalty points. It is, however, unfair to blame the court for this apparent injustice.

In cases involving death or serious injury where the charge is driving without due care and attention, the Crown Prosecution Service (CPS) will have considered all the circumstances before deciding that this charge is brought, rather than the more serious one of dangerous driving. Further, in the event of a death resulting, where the defendant had consumed alcohol to the extent that he was over the legal limit, the charge would have been causing death by careless driving while under the influence of drink or drugs.

What may amount to carelessness in one situation may

be considered prudent driving in another. For instance, you may be charged with careless driving in rush hour traffic, but might well not be prosecuted for a similar manoeuvre at 8 a.m. on a Sunday morning. Each case is unique. It is your driving at the relevant time that is pertinent, not what happened immediately before or after.

Defences

It is not a defence to careless driving that you did so through inexperience or error of judgement. Knowledge of your carelessness is not necessary. You may even be convicted of driving without due care if you carry out an emergency stop when commanded to do so by your driving instructor. It is your duty to ensure that it is safe to stop.

Police officers, fire officers and ambulance drivers are not exempt from prosecution for careless driving. It is accepted that such a driver owes the same duty of care to the public as any other driver. The court may, however, take account of the fact that the careless driving occurred while dealing with an emergency when sentencing for the offence.

It is a defence to careless driving if you satisfy the court that you did not depart from the standard of driving that would be exercised by a reasonable, prudent, competent driver in all the circumstances of your particular case.

It is a defence if you show that while you were driving you became temporarily incapable of controlling the car, for example through an epileptic fit or because you were attacked by a swarm of bees. Known as automatism, this defence is difficult to prove and you should seek legal advice. Self-induced automatism, e.g. through drink or drugs, is not a defence.

Your vehicle may have a mechanical defect of which you were unaware and it was not such a defect that you should reasonably have discovered. You will have to prove that there was a mechanical defect. Once you have done that it is up to the prosecution to show that you should have known about the defect. If the court is satisfied that there was a defect and that you did not know about that defect, you have a defence.

It is a defence if your careless driving is through necessity or duress. You have to prove that you drove carelessly in order to escape from an imminent threat of death or serious injury. No lesser threat will suffice.

Driving Without Reasonable Consideration

This is an offence which is proved if it is shown that other road users were inconvenienced by the manner of your driving.

What You Should Do

If you intend to plead guilty, there is little point in attending court. Plead guilty in absence. Write a letter setting out such points as you believe are in your favour. If no one was injured and damage was minimal, be sure the court is aware of that. If an accident occurred and your view was obstructed by a hedgerow or a parked vehicle, or if you were temporarily blinded while driving into the sun, say so. For examples of what you should write and what you should not say, see Chapter 10.

A typical example of carelessness, say driving out of a minor road and colliding with a vehicle on a main road, no injuries, minimal damage, may well be dealt with by way of a fine and licence endorsed with 6 penalty points. Running into the rear of the vehicle in front in rush hour traffic may well be regarded as less serious. The purpose of your letter is to persuade the court to impose a smaller fine, to order fewer penalty points.

Do not write anything which could have the opposite effect. For example, a motorist pleaded guilty to driving without due care and attention, and wrote to the court to the effect that he had no garage and that an accident occured because his windscreen was frosted over. This was not regarded with any favour by the magistrates. He was fined £250 and his licence was endorsed with 8 penalty points.

If you are confident that you have a defence to the charge, you should, of course, plead not guilty. You should be aware that **legal aid** is very unlikely to be granted for such offences. Unless you can afford to pay a solicitor, you will have to defend yourself. It is worth seeing the duty solicitor at the court on the day set aside for your trial. The duty solicitor will not represent you in court but will advise you how best to conduct your defence.

DRIVING OTHERWISE THAN IN ACCORDANCE WITH A LICENCE

On [date] at [place] you drove/caused to drive/permitted to drive a motor vehicle on a road otherwise than in accordance with a licence authorising you to drive a motor vehicle of that class.

Contrary to section 87 of the Road Traffic Act, 1988.

Maximum Penalty

Level 3 fine.

Fixed penalty available.

Facility to plead guilty in absence available.

Key Terms

■ **Legal aid** Legal representation either free of charge or upon payment of a small contribution

Whether the offence is endorsable or not depends on the circumstances.

- If the driving would not have been in accordance with any licence that could have been granted, the offence is endorsable.

- A provisional licence holder who drives unaccompanied by a qualified driver or who drives without L plates, commits an endorsable offence.

- A motorist who has held a full licence which has expired within the last ten years does not commit an endorsable offence.

When Endorsement Is Applicable

licence endorsed with 3 to 6 penalty points (Endorsement Code LC20);

disqualification from driving at the discretion of the court.

What You Should Do

If you are guilty of the offence and are offered the option of a **fixed penalty**, pay it, do not attend court. A court is likely to fine you more than the fixed penalty and order you to pay the costs of the prosecution.

If the offence is endorsable, the Fixed Penalty Office will endorse your driving licence with 3 points, while a court may order any number from 3 to 6.

Key Terms

■ **Fixed penalty** Provides an opportunity to have the matter dealt with other than by a court

If you are guilty and are not offered the option of a fixed penalty, plead guilty in absence. There is some risk of disqualification from driving especially when a provisional licence holder drives unaccompanied, but the court that hears your guilty plea in absence will not disqualify you. Do not attend court unless you receive an **adjournment notice** requiring you to do so.

If you intend to plead not guilty and your defence is that you had an appropriate driving licence at the date of the offence, there is no need to attend court. Simply send the licence to the court with your not guilty plea.

There is likely to be an alternative charge of failing to produce your driving licence to which you must plead either guilty or not guilty.

Causing or Permitting

The offence is committed if you cause or permit an unlicensed driver to drive. Whether or not you knew that the driver was not licensed to drive is irrelevant. Causing or permitting is not endorsable.

DRIVING WHILE DISQUALIFIED

On [date] at [place] being disqualified under Part 3 of the Road Traffic Act 1988 from holding or obtaining a licence to drive a motor vehicle you did drive a motor vehicle on a road.

Contrary to section 103 of the Road Traffic Act, 1988.

Key Terms

■ **Adjournment notice** A notice advising that the case has been adjourned to a particular date

Maximum Penalty

Level 5 fine and/or six months' imprisonment.

Endorsement with 6 penalty points (Endorsement Code BA10).

The court is likely to take a serious view if you commit the offence while on bail, or if you make any attempt to evade detection or arrest. Driving a long distance, driving on a number of occasions or driving a short time after disqualification are also adverse factors that the court will take into consideration when deciding on sentence.

Likely penalties include a substantial fine and/or a term of imprisonment. A probation order or a community service order are possibilities, as is an order of forfeiture of vehicle. The period of disqualification is likely to be extended.

A YOUNG MAN pleaded guilty to taking a vehicle without consent and he was granted bail for four weeks while a pre-sentence report was being prepared. At the same time, the court ordered an interim disqualification. The evening after he appeared in court he was arrested and charged with driving while disqualified. At the subsequent hearing he was sent to a young offenders' institution for three months and disqualified from driving for six months.

You must have been disqualified by a court. Driving after being refused a licence on the grounds of ill-health is not driving while disqualified. The prosecution must prove that you were driving or attempting to drive. It is not sufficient that you were in charge of a motor vehicle.

The offence of driving while disqualified is committed if you have been disqualified until you pass a driving test and, though you have a provisional licence, you fail to comply with the conditions of that licence, e.g. you drive without L plates, or without qualified supervision or on a motorway. It is not a defence to the charge that you were unaware of the disqualification.

A person driving while disqualified cannot, in law, have insurance cover. The prosecution will almost invariably bring two charges, driving while disqualified and using a vehicle without insurance.

The disqualification from driving applies to the roads of Great Britain. You may drive outside Great Britain provided you comply with the laws of the country in which you are driving.

Prosecution for this offence does not have to be brought within six months of the date the offence was committed, but within six months of the offence coming to the notice of the police.

Defences

1. Mistaken identity. It wasn't you.

2. The vehicle was not a motor vehicle.

3. The offence was not committed on a road.

4. You are not a disqualified driver: you have not been dis- qualified by a court.

What You Should Do

When you were disqualified you would have been told by the court that the period of disqualification begins immediately and that, if you drive a motor vehicle on the roads of Great Britain during the period of disqualification, you commit an offence for which you may be sent to prison.

If you do drive, are caught and charged with this offence, you should not be too surprised if the sentence of the court is, indeed, imprisonment.

You should consult a solicitor or see the duty solicitor on the date of your court appearance.

If this was an isolated incident, make sure that the court is aware of that. If you drove only a short distance, be sure the court knows that. If you drove safely, were not involved in an accident and committed no moving traffic offence, make that clear to the magistrates. Explain why you were driving.

The court will be considering increasing the period of disqualification. Point out the effect that this would have on your work or your ability to find work.

A MOTORIST was disqualified for six months under the totting-up provisions. A few days before the period of disqualification ended, he thought it would be a good idea to remove his car from his garage and drive it down the road 'just to be sure that it was all right'. Stopped by the police, he was charged with driving while disqualified and with driving without insurance.

He was fined a total of £480, had to pay £30 prosecution costs and had his licence endorsed with 6 penalty points for the first offence and 8 for the second. The court did not extend the period of disqualification.

Because both charges arose from the same incident, the effective number of penalty points imposed was 8, not 14, but he was well on his way towards 12 penalty points and disqualification from driving under the totting-up provisions.

Special Reasons for Not Endorsing Your Licence

In certain limited circumstances the court may be persuaded to find special reasons for not endorsing your driving licence:

1. the fact that you drove a short distance in circumstances where you were unlikely to come into contact with other road users;

2. the fact that you committed the offence while coping with a real emergency.

A DISQUALIFIED driver went to the cinema with his wife. On returning to her car, she found that she was unable to manoeuvre it out of the cinema car park. Her husband managed to extricate the vehicle and parked it on the road. Observed by a police officer, he was charged with driving while disqualified. He was convicted but the court found special reasons for not endorsing his driving licence.

Special reasons are best argued by a solicitor. For a fuller account see Chapter 10.

NO INSURANCE

On [date] at [place] you did use a motor vehicle there not being in force in relation to the use of the said vehicle such a policy of insurance or such a security in respect of third party risks as complies with the requirements of Part 6 of the Road Traffic Act, 1988.

Contrary to section 143 of the Road Traffic Act, 1988.

Key Terms

■ **Special reasons** Reasons special to the circumstances of the offence which allow a court a discretion not to endorse or not to disqualify

Maximum Penalty

Level 4 fine, obligatory endorsement with 6 to 8 penalty points.

Disqualification at the discretion of the court.

Endorsement Code IN10.

Note that the word used in the charge is not 'driving' but 'using' a motor vehicle. There must be an element of controlling, managing or operating the vehicle, but the vehicle may be stationary and unattended on the road.

A passenger may be charged with 'using'. An example might be the owner of a vehicle who sits beside an uninsured driver or any passenger in a vehicle who is engaged in a joint enterprise with a driver who is uninsured.

When deciding on a penalty, the court will have in mind the length of time that the vehicle had been uninsured and how much it would have cost to insure the vehicle, whether the offence was committed deliberately or through some accidental oversight.

If you deliberately drive without insurance, i.e. if you drive knowing that you are uninsured, you are at high risk of a period of disqualification from driving.

THE OWNER of a minicab admitted using the vehicle without insurance. He said that a few weeks before the offence he had changed his address. He had overlooked the fact that his insurance had expired and had not received a renewal notice. He asked the court not to disqualify him as driving the cab represented his only source of income.

He was fined £600 and his driving licence was endorsed with 6 penalty points.

You must be particularly careful when driving someone else's vehicle with their permission. It is not sufficient that the other person tells you that you are covered by the other person's insurance. Ask to see the certificate. Similarly, if you drive someone else's vehicle believing that you are covered by your own insurance, you must be very sure that this is the case.

Compensation

The court has the power to award compensation for injury or damage as a result of an accident. Most commonly compensation is ordered where an uninsured driver is involved in an accident and the other party has an excess on their policy, i.e. the driver is required to pay the first, say, £100 of any claim. The uninsured driver may be ordered to pay this excess.

Compensation is not, however, restricted to such a small sum as a magistrates' court has the power to award compensation up to a maximum of £5000 for each offence. In practice, claims for large sums are usually pursued through the civil courts.

Defences

This is an absolute offence. Either you were insured or you were not. Apart from mistaken identity, there is only one defence, as follows. If an employee uses a vehicle in the course of employment and it subsequently becomes apparent that he or she was uninsured, it is a defence if the employee shows:

1. that the vehicle neither belonged to, nor was hired or rented by, him or her;

2. that the employee was using it in the course of his or her employment;

3. that he or she neither knew nor had any reason to believe that the vehicle was uninsured.

What You Should Do

If you had insurance which was valid on the relevant date, you should either send the certificate to the court with a not guilty plea or attend court on the date shown on the summons, plead not guilty and produce the certificate. You must produce the original, as a photocopy or fax is not sufficient. If you need more time to trace the document, ask for an adjournment. Provided the prosecution find the document in order, you will not be convicted.

If you intend to plead guilty, you are unlikely to be given the opportunity to do so in absence. If, however, a **guilty in absence** form is included in the documents accompanying the summons, take advantage of it. Do not attend court. Write and explain why you were using the vehicle without insurance.

If no guilty in absence form is included or if, having written to the court, you receive a notice requiring you to attend for consideration of disqualification, you must attend court. If you do not, a warrant for your arrest will almost certainly be issued.

If you are to have any chance of avoiding disqualification for this offence, you must be able to show that you did not commit the offence deliberately, i.e. that you did not use the vehicle knowing that you were uninsured. Much depends on the circumstances. If you can show that the offence was committed through an accidental oversight or a mistaken belief that you were insured when you were not, or even that your insurance had recently expired, you may have some chance of avoiding disqualification.

Key Terms

■ **Guilty in absence** A guilty plea by post or otherwise in the absence of the defendant

Causing or Permitting

Precisely the same penalties apply to a person causing or permitting the driver to commit the above offence. The charge will then read:

. . . did cause to be used by . . ./did permit to be used by . . .

Causing arises if you cause the journey to be made without enquiring whether the driver is insured. 'Please take me in your car.' Permitting arises when you allow someone to drive your vehicle either:

1. knowing he or she is not insured;

2. suspecting he or she is not insured;

3. not knowing but not taking steps to establish whether or not he or she is insured;

4. enquiring about this but not sufficiently.

An honest and genuine belief that the other person is insured is not a defence. Neither do you have to own the vehicle you permit someone to drive. If you give permission to an uninsured person to use a vehicle, perhaps your father's vehicle or one that you have rented, you commit an offence.

⚠ A COUPLE took the train to Cornwall for a holiday. The husband decided to rent a car for a few days. He paid the rental charge which included a sum for insurance. He arranged with the rental company that he would be the only driver. The next day, he allowed his wife to drive. The vehicle was involved in an accident. She was not insured, was charged with using a vehicle without insurance and he was charged with permitting.

Defences

1. You did not give permission, implied or otherwise.

2. You gave permission on the express condition that the person would first insure the vehicle or only if he or she was insured to drive it.

Special Reasons for Not Endorsing

There are circumstances in which, although you plead guilty to the offence, the court may find **special reasons** for not endorsing your driving livence:

1. the fact that you drove a very short distance in circumstances where you were unlikely to come into contact with other road users;

2. the fact that you committed the offence while coping with a real emergency;

3. the fact that you were misled into believing that you were insured, that a layperson reading the terms of the policy might genuinely, but mistakenly, believe that he or she was insured.

A DEFENDANT had a driving licence but no car. When his wife went into labour, he borrowed his neighbour's car to take her to the nearest maternity unit. He was not insured but the court found special reasons for not endorsing his licence.

Key Terms

■ **Special reasons** Reasons special to the circumstances of the offence which allow a court a discretion not to endorse or not to disqualify

If you believe that you may have special reasons for not endorsing, you are well advised to consult a solicitor or see the duty solicitor on the day of the hearing. For a fuller account of special reasons, see Chapter 10.

LEAVING A VEHICLE IN A DANGEROUS POSITION

On [date] at [place] being a person in charge of a vehicle namely . . . did cause/permit said vehicle/a trailer drawn by said vehicle to remain at rest on a road in such a position/in such a condition/in such circumstances as to involve a danger of injury to other persons using the road.

Contrary to section 22 of the Road Traffic Act, 1988 (as amended by Schedule 4 of the Road Traffic Act, 1991).

Maximum Penalty

Level 3 fine.

Licence endorsed with 3 penalty points.

Endorsement Code MS10.

Disqualification from driving at the discretion of the court.

Fixed penalty available.

Guilty in absence procedure available.

If you park a vehicle or trailer on a road in such a position or in such a condition that danger is likely to be caused to other road users, you commit an offence.

Examples of places where you should not park are given in the Highway Code and include:

- at or near a school entrance;
- at or near a bus stop or taxi rank;
- within 10 m of a junction;
- near the brow of a hill;
- opposite a traffic island;
- on the approach to a pedestrian crossing.

A vehicle which was earlier involved in an accident and is parked with, for example, a wing hanging off, may be parked 'in such a condition that danger is likely to be caused'.

You should know that a local authority has the power to remove a vehicle left in a dangerous position.

What You Should Do

If you are guilty of the offence and are offered the option of paying a fixed penalty, pay it. If you receive a summons and intend to plead guilty, do so in absence. Do not attend court unless you receive a notice requiring you to do so.

LOAD, INSECURE

On [date] at [place] you did use a motor vehicle, on which was carried a load which was not so secured, if necessary by physical restraint other than its own weight and be in such a position that neither danger nor nuisance is likely to be caused to any person or property by reason of the load or any part thereof falling or being blown from the vehicle or by reason of any other movement of the load or any part thereof in relation to the vehicle.

Contrary to Regulation 100 of the Road Vehicles Construction and Use Regulations, 1986 and section 40A of the Road Traffic Act, 1988.

Maximum Penalty

Level 4 fine (goods vehicles Level 5 fine).

Licence endorsed with 3 penalty points.

Endorsement Code CU50.

Disqualification from driving at the discretion of the court.

No fixed penalty available.

Facility to plead guilty in absence available.

The fine imposed by a court will reflect the degree of danger caused by the insecure load.

The offence is committed if the load, or part of the load, falls from the vehicle. The offence may be committed even if the load has not moved or has only moved in such a way as to remain on the vehicle. Whether or not a load is insecure in these circumstances is a matter which the court must decide.

This is an offence of strict liability. Either the load was insecure or it was not.

It is not a defence that the driver was not responsible for loading the vehicle. It is not a defence that the driver did not know and had no reason to suspect that the load was insecure. **Special reasons** for not **endorsing** may, however, be argued in these circumstances.

Key Terms

■ **Special reasons** Reasons special to the circumstances of the offence which allow a court a discretion not to endorse or not to disqualify ■ **Endorsement** The annotation of your driving licence with penalty points

What You Should Do

If you intend to plead guilty but believe you may have special reasons for not endorsing, you will have to attend court and give evidence on oath. Special reasons are best argued by a solicitor. Either consult a solicitor or see the **duty solicitor** on the day of your court appearance.

If you intend to plead guilty and do not intend to put forward special reasons, there is no need to attend court. Plead guilty in absence. Write a letter to the court explaining why the load was insecure.

PEDESTRIAN CROSSING OFFENCES

Zebra Crossings

Failing to give precedence

On [date] at [place] being the driver of a vehicle namely . . . failed to accord precedence to a foot passenger on the carriageway within the limits of an uncontrolled zebra crossing on [location] the said foot passenger being on the carriageway within the said limits before the vehicle or any part thereof had come on to the carriageway within those limits.

Contrary to Regulation 8 of the 'Zebra' Pedestrian Crossing Regulations, 1971, section 25(5) of the Road Traffic Regulations Act, 1984 and Schedule 2 of the Road Traffic Offenders Act, 1988.

> ### Key Terms
> ■ **Duty solicitor** A solicitor available to give advice without charge to defendants in court

Overtaking within limits

On [date] at [place] being the driver of a vehicle namely . . . which or part of which was within a zebra controlled area on [location] and which was proceeding towards the limits of an uncontrolled zebra crossing in relation to which that area was indicated, caused the said vehicle or a part thereof to pass ahead of the foremost part of [another moving motor vehicle being a vehicle proceeding in the same direction wholly or partly in that area/a stationary vehicle which was stopped on the same side of the crossing as your vehicle for the purpose of according precedence to a foot passenger].

Contrary to Regulation 10 of the 'Zebra' Pedestrian Crossing Regulations etc., etc.

Waiting within the limits

On [date] at [place] being the driver of a vehicle namely . . . caused the same or part thereof to stop within the limits of a zebra crossing on [location].

Contrary to Regulation 9(1) of the 'Zebra' Pedestrian Crossing Regulations etc., etc.

Stopping in area adjacent to crossing

On [date] at [place] being the driver of a vehicle namely . . . caused the same or part thereof to stop in a zebra controlled area on [location].

Contrary to Regulation 12(2) of the 'Zebra' Crossing Regulations etc., etc.

Maximum Penalty

Level 3 fine.

Licence endorsed with 3 penalty points.

Endorsement Code PC20.

Disqualification at the discretion of the court.

Fixed penalty available.

Guilty in absence procedure available.

You commit an offence in the following circumstances.

- If you fail to give precedence to a pedestrian who is already on the crossing. Where there is a central reservation, each side counts as a separate crossing. The pedestrian may not remain on the crossing any longer than is necessary to cross from side to side. A person pushing a bicycle is a pedestrian.

- If you overtake another vehicle within the limits of a zebra crossing. The vehicle you overtake does not have to be a motor vehicle (it may, for example, be a bicycle) and you commit the offence whether the vehicle is moving or stationary provided that, if it is stationary, it has stopped in order to allow a pedestrian to cross.

- If you park a vehicle or any part of a vehicle on the approach to a zebra crossing. The limits of a crossing are indicated by marks or studs on the highway, and the size, colour and type of such markings must comply with pedestrian crossing regulations.

Pelican Crossings

Driver failing to stop when red light is showing

On [date] at [place] being the driver of a vehicle namely . . . at a time when the vehicular light signal at a 'pelican' crossing on [location] was showing a red light caused the said vehicle or part thereof to proceed beyond [the stop line/post or other structure on which was mounted the primary signal facing you on the side of the carriageway on which you approached the crossing].

Contrary to Regulation 16 of the 'Pelican' Crossing Regulations and General Directions, 1987, section 25(5) of the Road Traffic Regulations Act, 1984 and Schedule 2 of the Road Traffic Offenders Act, 1988. (Code PC20)

Failing to give precedence to a pedestrian

On [date] at [place] being the driver of a vehicle namely . . . at a time when the vehicular traffic light signal at a 'pelican' crossing was showing a flashing amber light failed to accord precedence to a pedestrian within the limits of that crossing the said pedestrian being on [the carriageway/central reservation] within the said limits before any part of the vehicle had entered those limits.

Contrary to Regulation 17, etc., etc. (Code PC30)

Overtaking within limits

On [date] at [place] being the driver of a vehicle namely . . . which or part of which was within a 'pelican' crossing controlled area on [location] and which was proceeding towards the limits of a 'pelican' crossing in relation to which the area was indicated caused the said vehicle or a part thereof to pass ahead of the foremost part of [1. another moving vehicle being a vehicle proceeding in the same direction wholly or partly within that area/2. a stationary vehicle which was stopped on the same side of the crossing as your vehicle] for the purpose of [according preference to a pedestrian/conforming to a vehicular traffic light showing a red light].

Contrary to Regulation 19, etc., etc. (Code PC20)

Waiting within limits

On [date] at [place] being the driver of a vehicle namely . . . caused the same or part thereof to stop within the limits of a 'pelican' crossing on [location].

Contrary to Regulation 18(1), etc., etc. (Code PC20)

Stopping in area adjacent to a crossing

On [date] at [place] being the driver of a vehicle namely . . . caused the same or part thereof to stop in a 'pelican' controlled area on [location].

Contrary to Regulation 12(a), etc., etc. (Code PC20)

Maximum Penalty

Level 3 fine.

Licence endorsed with 3 penalty points.

Disqualification at the discretion of the court.

Fixed penalty available.

Guilty plea in absence procedure available.

At 'pelican' crossings, the red stop light is followed by an amber flashing light. When the amber light is flashing, you are still required to give way to pedestrians. Unlike 'zebra' crossings, a 'pelican' crossing is one crossing, even though there may be a central reservation, and you must give precedence to pedestrians crossing from the other side of the reservation.

As with 'zebra' crossings, you commit an offence if you overtake or park on the crossing, or on the approach to the crossing.

Exceptions

1. A vehicle may stop in a 'pelican' controlled area for the purpose of making a left or right turn.

2. A public service vehicle being used to provide a local service or carrying passengers for hire or reward may stop in a 'pelican' controlled area only so long as is necessary to take up or set down passengers.

School Crossings

On [date] at [place] at a time between the hours of eight in the morning and half past five in the afternoon being the [driver of/person propelling] a vehicle namely . . . approaching a place on [location] where children on their way to and from school were crossing or seeking to cross the road and having been required to stop the said vehicle by a school crossing patrol wearing an approved uniform and exhibiting a prescribed sign [failed to do so before reaching the said place and so as not to stop or impede the children crossing/put the vehicle in motion again so as to reach the said place whilst the sign was still being exhibited].

Contrary to Regulation 28(3) of the Road Traffic Regulation Act, 1984 and Schedule 2 of the Road Traffic Offenders Act, 1988.

Maximum Penalty

Level 3 fine.

Licence endorsed with 3 penalty points.

Endorsement Code PC30.

Disqualification at the discretion of the court.

Fixed penalty available.

Guilty in absence procedure available.

Note that the offence may only be committed between certain time limits, and that the patrol must be wearing an approved uniform and carrying a prescribed sign. At present an approved uniform is a white coat and the prescribed sign is a 'stop' sign of a specified size and shape.

The children must be on their way to and from school or on their way from one part of school to another.

The offence is considered more serious than other crossing offences because of the vulnerability of those using the crossing. While disqualification from driving for other pedestrian crossing offences is rare, if you are convicted by a court of this offence disqualification becomes a real possibility.

What You Should Do

If you are given the option of paying a **fixed penalty** and intend to plead guilty, accept the fixed penalty. If you are not offered the option of a fixed penalty or, for some reason, are unable to take advantage of that option, plead guilty in absence.

Write a letter to the court. If no one was injured, make that clear to the magistrates. If you believe that you were too close to the crossing when the 'lollipop person' stepped out into the road, tell the court.

If, despite your letter, you receive an **adjournment notice** requiring you to attend for consideration of disqualification, you will have to attend court. See the duty solicitor, and advise him what effect disqualification from driving will have on your work or your ability to find work. The solicitor will address the magistrates on your behalf.

Key Terms

■ **Fixed penalty** Provides an opportunity to have the matter dealt with other than by a court ■ **Adjournment notice** A notice advising that the case has been adjourned to a particular date

SPEEDING, EXCEEDING THE SPEED LIMIT

On [date] at [place] you did drive a motor vehicle on a restricted road at a speed exceeding 30 m.p.h.

Contrary to sections 81 and 89 of the Road Traffic Regulation Act, 1984.

[   ] you did drive a motor vehicle at a speed exceeding 40/50/60/70 m.p.h., that being the limit of speed specified in respect of that road in an Order made under section 84 or 88 Road Traffic Regulation Act, 1984.

Contrary to sections 84 and 89 of the Road Traffic Regulation Act, 1984.

[   ] you did drive a goods vehicle on a road at a speed greater than [   ] m.p.h., the speed specified in Schedule 6 of the Road Traffic Regulation Act, 1984 as the maximum speed specified in Schedule 6 of the Road Traffic Regulation Act, 1984 as the maximum speed in regard of a vehicle of that class.

Contrary to sections 86 and 89 of the Road Traffic Regulation Act, 1984.

Maximum Penalty

Level 3 fine.

Licence endorsed with between 3 and 6 penalty points.

Endorsement Code SP30.

Disqualification from driving at the discretion of the court.

You are at high risk of disqualification from driving if you drive at a speed of 30 m.p.h. or more over the limit.

There is some risk even at lesser speeds.

What You Should Do

If you are given the option of paying a **fixed penalty** and are guilty of the offence, do not even think about being dealt with by a court (unless you think you have special reasons). The Fixed Penalty Office will endorse your licence with the minimum number of penalty points, i.e. 3. A court may order any number from 3 to 6 and may impose a fine substantially greater than the fixed penalty plus prosecution costs.

A MOTORIST was stopped by the police who alleged that he was driving at a speed of 62.5 m.p.h. on a road where speed was restricted to 40 m.p.h. A fixed penalty notice was issued and it was explained to the motorist that he had the option of attending court. The motorist attended court and pleaded guilty. He was fined £80 and his licence was endorsed with 5 penalty points.

Had he accepted the fixed penalty, the fine, at the time, would have been £40 and his licence would have been endorsed with 3 penalty points.

If you are offered the option of paying a fixed penalty but for some reason you are not able to take advantage of that offer and you receive a summons, be sure that the court is aware that a fixed penalty was offered. Give the reasons why you were not able to take advantage of the offer.

Key Terms

■ **Fixed penalty** Provides an opportunity to have the matter dealt with other than by a court

⚠️ A MOTORIST was stopped by the police and it was alleged that he was driving at 47.6 m.p.h. in a 30 m.p.h. limit. He did not have his driving documents with him and was required to produce them at a police station within seven days. He could not find his driving licence and was unable to take advantage of the offer of a fixed penalty. He received a summons for the speeding offence and for failing to produce his driving licence.

He found his driving licence and sent it to the court together with a plea of guilty to both offences. He explained that he had temporarily mislaid the licence and had been unable to take advantage of the fixed penalty. For the speeding offence, the magistrates took a lenient view and fined him £40, licence endorsed with 3 penalty points.

If you receive a summons and intend to plead guilty, always plead guilty in absence (unless you intend to plead special reasons for not endorsing). Even if you exceeded the speed limit by such a margin that you fear disqualification from driving, write to the court: you have nothing to lose.

A court that hears your guilty plea in absence will not disqualify you.

Only attend court if you receive an adjournment notice requiring you to do so for consideration of disqualification.

When writing to the court, if you had a good reason for speeding, give that reason. If traffic was light, and weather and visibility good, be sure the court is aware of that. (See Chapter 10 for more on writing letters to court.)

If you are charged with two offences and plead guilty to the more serious one, the prosecution may be persuaded to withdraw the second charge.

⚠️ A MOTORIST received a summons alleging driving without due care and attention and exceeding the speed limit. The fact that the motorist was driving at a speed in excess of the legal limit was a factor in the careless driving charge. When the motorist pleaded guilty to the more serious offence, the speeding charge was withdrawn.

Defences

1. You were not exceeding the speed limit.

2. Mistaken identity – it wasn't you.

3. You were driving an exempted vehicle in an emergency (for exempted vehicles, see below).

You cannot be convicted on the evidence of one witness alone. The evidence of such a witness will have to be **corroborated**. Corroboration is provided, for example, by the speedomoter reading of a police car, by radar equipment or **Vascar**, or by a second police officer. Factual evidence, e.g. skid marks or damage, may amount to corroboration.

Motorists will often plead not guilty to exceeding the speed limit when the statement of facts alleges a speed of (say) 55 m.p.h. in a 30 m.p.h. limit and then readily admit that they were driving at 40 m.p.h. A little thought will make it apparent that this is not sensible. The correct course is to plead guilty but to challenge the police evidence of the speed.

While traffic patrol cars are equipped with, for example, a **police pilot**, Panda cars are not. You may well be speeding, but if it is alleged by the driver of a Panda car that you drove at a speed of, say, 60 m.p.h. on a road where speed is restricted to 30 m.p.h., you may persuade a court that there is some small margin for error.

Key Terms

■ **Corrobation** Separate and additional evidence supporting or confirming the main evidence ■ **Vascar, police pilot** Computer devices which calculate average speed over a measured time and distance

⚠ A POLICE OFFICER, sitting in a Panda car off the road, saw a car go by and, forming the impression that its speed exceeded 30 m.p.h., he gave chase and caused the vehicle to stop. A summons was issued alleging a speed of 61 m.p.h. Fearing disqualification if the allegation was proved the motorist wrote to the court and pleaded guilty, but insisted that the speed of his vehicle did not exceed 56 m.p.h. The magistrates gave him the benefit of the doubt.

He was fined £100 and his licence was endorsed with 6 penalty points. He was not disqualified.

Special Reasons for Not Endorsing

If you commit the offence while responding to a true emergency, you may have special reasons for not having your licence endorsed.

⚠ A SHOPKEEPER received a telephone call from the police in the middle of the night advising him that his premises had been broken into and, while hurrying to the scene, he drove at 65 m.p.h. on a road where speed was restricted to 40 m.p.h. He was stopped by the police and a fixed penalty notice was issued. He declined the offer of a fixed penalty, received a summons and pleaded guilty. His solicitor successfully argued special reasons for not endorsing.

If you wish to plead special reasons for not endorsing, you must attend court. You should either consult a solicitor or make use of the **duty solicitor** scheme.

Key Terms

■ **Duty solicitor** A solicitor available to give advice without charge to defendants in court

Inciting the Commission of the Offence

If an employer of a driver issues timetables or gives instructions that a journey is to be completed within a certain time (which is shown to be impracticable without an offence of speeding being committed), the employer could be convicted of inciting the commission of the offence.

Exemptions

The following vehicles are exempt:

- vehicles being used for fire brigade, ambulance or police purposes, but only when to keep to the speed limit would hinder the purpose for which they are being used on that occasion;

- vehicles owned by the Secretary of State for Defence, and used for naval, military or airforce purposes, and constructed or adapted for combative purposes or training etc.

- ## TRAFFIC LIGHTS, FAILING TO COMPLY WITH

- ## POLICE/TRAFFIC SIGNS, FAILING TO COMPLY WITH

- ## USING A VEHICLE IN A DANGEROUS CONDITION

These are offences for which a **fixed penalty** is available. If you are guilty of the offence, pay the fixed penalty. If you receive a **summons**, there is no need to attend court; plead guilty by letter. For using a vehicle in a dangerous condition, a **VDRS notice** may be issued. Take advantage of that option.

Key Terms

■ **Fixed penalty** Provides an opportunity to have the matter dealt with other than by a court ■ **Summons** The document which begins most court proceedings ■ **VDRS** A scheme whereby a motorist is given an opportunity to put right vehicle defects without penalty

Motorway Offences

Most of the offences described in this book may be committed on a motorway just as they may be committed on any other road. There are, however, a number of offences which may only be committed on a motorway.

The most common of these are:

exceeding the 70 m.p.h. speed limit

exceeding the speed limit in a contraflow system

stopping on the hard shoulder

driving on the central reservation or on the hard shoulder

driving in reverse

driving in the wrong direction

being a learner driver on the motorway

making a U-turn

driving an unauthorised vehicle in the third lane

driving in contravention to traffic signs (e.g. traffic light, halt signs)

These are all offences for which a **fixed penalty** is available. If you are offered that option, unless you are confident that

---

Key Terms

■ **Fixed penalty** Provides an opportunity to have the matter dealt with other than by a court

you have a defence to the charge, do not even think about having the matter dealt with by a court but pay the fixed penalty. If you are offered the option of paying a fixed penalty but are unable to take advantage of that offer, receive a summons and then plead guilty by letter, be sure you make the court aware that the offer of a fixed penalty was made and explain why you were unable to take advantage of that offer.

EXCEEDING THE SPEED LIMIT

On [date] at [place] you did drive a vehicle on the . . . motorway at a speed exceeding 70 m.p.h., that being the limit of speed specified in Regulation 3 of the Motorways Traffic (Speed Limit) Regulations, 1974.

Maximum Penality

Level 4 fine

Endorsement with between 3 and 6 penalty points

Endorsement Code SP50

Disqualification at the discretion of the court.

You are likely to be offered the option of paying a fixed penalty where it is alleged that the speed recorded was in the 80s. When the speed alleged is in the 90s and you receive a summons, upon conviction you will have to pay a fine somewhat higher than the fixed penalty and the number of penalty points ordered is likely to be 5 or 6. You are at some risk of being disqualified from driving for a short period.

If you drive on a motorway at a speed of 100 m.p.h. or more, you are at high risk of disqualification from driving.

If you receive a summons for exceeding the speed limit and you intend to plead guilty, even if the speed alleged is 100 m.p.h., you should plead guilty in absence. (For what to write and what not to write, see Chapter 10.) You have nothing to lose, as the court which hears your guilty plea in absence will not disqualify you.

If you receive a notice requiring you to attend court because that court has adjourned your case for consideration of disqualification, your chances of avoiding such a penalty will not be good.

Each case is different – a different time of the day, different traffic conditions, different visibility or weather conditions – but the likely periods of disqualification are as follows:

100/105 m.p.h.	*7 days*
106/110 m.p.h.	*14 days*
111/115 m.p.h.	*21 days*

Above such speeds the period of disqualification is likely to increase sharply.

A DEFENDANT was driving his BMW saloon on a motorway in the early hours of the morning at a speed of about 90 m.p.h. when he was overtaken by a Sierra Cosworth driven at about 130 m.p.h. His motives for giving chase are not clear but he finally caught up with the Cosworth and passed it at a speed of 135 m.p.h. – only to find that it was an unmarked police car . . .

He was fined £400 and disqualified from driving for four months.

When you attend court for consideration of disqualification, the court will hear the facts of the case and you will be asked if you wish to say anything. It is unlikely that the effect of disqualification for a short period will be that you will lose your job. If there is any possibility of that, however, it is essential that you produce documentary evidence, for example a letter from your employer.

If you are self-employed, it is unlikely that the effect of a short period of disqualification will be catastrophic. Can you make other arrangements? Could you employ a driver or get your partner to drive you?

You should, nevertheless, make an effort to persuade the magistrates either not to disqualify you or to disqualify you for a shorter period.

If traffic was light, and weather conditions and visibility good, be sure to point that out to the court. Why were you speeding? If you had a good reason, tell the court. If, on reflection, your reason for speeding was not so good, it is better not to give a reason at all. (For what to say and what not to say, see Chapter 10.)

EXCEEDING THE SPEED LIMIT IN A CONTRAFLOW SYSTEM

That you on [date] at . . . motorway drove a motor vehicle on a road in contravention of sub-section (1) (b) of the 70 miles per hour, 60 miles per hour and 50 miles per hour (Temporary Speed Limits) Order 1977.

Contrary to section 88 of the Road Traffic Regulation Act, 1984.

Maximum Penalty

Level 4 fine

Licence endorsed with 3 to 6 penalty points

Endorsement Code SP60

Disqualification at the discretion of the court.

Mandatory temporary speed limits must be clearly marked with the maximum speed. If you exceed the temporary limit and exceed 70 m.p.h., you will be charged with exceeding the 70 m.p.h. speed limit.

You cannot be convicted of this offence solely on the evidence of one witness who says that, in their opinion, you were exceeding the temporary speed limit. **Corroboration** is necessary (see page 102).

STOPPING ON THE HARD SHOULDER

On [date] at [place] you did stop or allow to remain at rest for longer than was necessary a certain vehicle namely . . . on the hard shoulder of the motorway.

Contrary to section 17(4) of the Road Traffic Regulation Act, 1984.

Maximum Penalty

Level 4 fine, not endorsable.

You may not stop your vehicle on the hard shoulder except in the following circumstances:

1. because of breakdown, lack of fuel, oil or water;

2. through an accident, illness or other emergency;

Key Terms

■ **Corroboration** Separate and additional evidence supporting or confirming the main evidence

3. to permit the driver or a passenger to recover or move an object which has fallen on the motorway;

4. to permit any person to give assistance in any of the above.

Your vehicle must not remain on the hard shoulder for any longer than is necessary and, as far as is reasonably practicable, it must not be parked in such a way as to cause danger to other road users.

A POLICE PATROL came across a car parked on the hard shoulder in the early hours of the morning. The driver was asleep. He was charged with stopping on the hard shoulder and pleaded not guilty. In evidence he said that he felt too tired to drive any further and believed that by continuing to drive he would have been a danger to other road users. He was convicted and fined £120.

A subsequent appeal to the Crown Court was dismissed. The judge commented that, in the circumstances described, it was necessary to leave the motorway at a convenient junction.

Defences

1. That you stopped in an emergency, such as one of the circumstances described above. An accident need not necessarily involve your vehicle – the carriageway could be blocked due to an accident ahead. Neither need it be the driver who is ill. A passenger may, for example, be suffering from travel sickness and wish to vomit or may have suffered an epileptic fit etc.

2. That your vehicle was moved as soon as practicable. Depending on the circumstances, this may be within a matter of minutes or a matter of hours.

DRIVING ON THE CENTRAL RESERVATION OR HARD SHOULDER

On [date] at [place] you drove a motor vehicle/lorry/coach etc. on a part of the motorway which was not a carriageway.

Contrary to section 17(4) of the Road Traffic Regulation Act, 1984.

Maximum Penalty

Level 4 fine

Licence endorsed with 3 penalty points

Endorsement Code MW10

Disqualification at the discretion of the court.

No vehicle may be driven on the central reservation. No vehicle may be driven on the hard shoulder except in the circumstances outlined on pages 110–11.

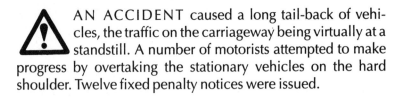 AN ACCIDENT caused a long tail-back of vehicles, the traffic on the carriageway being virtually at a standstill. A number of motorists attempted to make progress by overtaking the stationary vehicles on the hard shoulder. Twelve fixed penalty notices were issued.

Defences

1. That you were complying with a traffic sign or acting with the permission of a constable in uniform.

2. That you drove on the central reservation or on the hard shoulder in order to avoid an accident or in an emergency and that you acted in such a manner as to cause as little danger or inconvenience to other traffic as possible.

DRIVING IN REVERSE

On [date] at [time] you did drive/move a certain vehicle, namely . . . backwards on the carriageway of the motorway.

Contrary to section 17(4) of the Road Traffic Regulation Act, 1984.

Maximum Penalty

Level 4 fine

Licence endorsed with 3 penalty points (Endorsement Code MW10)

Disqualification at the discretion of the court.

Defences

1. It was necessary to reverse in order to proceed forward again or to be connected to another vehicle.
2. That you reversed in order to avoid an accident or in an emergency and that you acted in such a manner as to cause as little danger or inconvenience to other road users as possible.

DRIVING IN THE WRONG DIRECTION

On [date] at [place] you did drive a motor vehicle namely . . . on a length of carriageway contiguous to the central reservation in a direction otherwise than so that the central reservation was at all times on the right hand or offside of the vehicle.

Contrary to section 17(4) of the Road Traffic Regulation Act, 1984.

Maximum Penalty

Level 4 fine

Licence endorsed with 3 penalty points

Endorsement Code MW10

Disqualification at the discretion of the court.

In practice, the prosecution are likely to bring the more serious charge of dangerous driving. Although a fixed penalty is possible, you will be very fortunate to be offered that option. Upon conviction before a court, the magistrates will give serious thought to disqualification and you may be ordered to take a driving test.

The sentence of the court will reflect the distance driven and the reason you give for driving in the wrong direction. Evidence of drinking will be an aggravating factor.

Defence

That you were complying with a traffic sign or acting on the instruction of a constable in uniform.

BEING A LEARNER DRIVER ON A MOTORWAY

On [date] at [place] being the holder of a provisional licence and not having passed the appropriate test, you did drive a certain vehicle, namely . . . on the motorway.

Contrary to section 17(4) of the Road Traffic Regulation Act, 1984.

Maximum Penalty

Level 4 fine

Licence endorsed with 3 penalty points

Endorsement Code MW10

Disqualification at the discretion of the court.

MAKING A U-TURN ON A MOTORWAY

On [date] at . . . motorway you did drive on a length of carriageway (being a length which is not contiguous to a central reservation) which can be entered at one end only by vehicles driven in one direction only, or moved or caused to be moved a motor vehicle so as to cause it to turn and proceed in or face the opposite direction.

Contrary to section 15 of the Road Traffic Regulation Act, 1984.

Maximum Penalty

Level 4 fine

Licence endorsed with 3 penalty points

Endorsement Code MW10

Disqualification at the discretion of the court.

The prosecution are likely to charge you with driving without due care and attention or even with dangerous driving.

You are at high risk of disqualification upon conviction for this offence. You should give your reason for this manoeuvre. If traffic was light and visibility good, be sure the court is aware of that.

Defence

That you acted so as to avoid an accident or in an emergency and in such a manner as to cause as little danger as possible to other road users.

DRIVING AN UNAUTHORISED VEHICLE IN THE THIRD LANE

On [date] at [place] you did drive/stop or cause to remain at rest a motor vehicle namely . . . on the right-hand or off-side lane of a length of carriageway which had three or more traffic lanes at a place where all three lanes were open for use by traffic proceeding in the same direction.

Contrary to section 17(4) of the Road Traffic Regulation Act, 1984.

Maximum Penalty

Level 4 fine

Licence endorsed with 3 penalty points

Disqualification at the discretion of the court.

A number of vehicles are not allowed to use the right-hand or off-side lane of a three-lane motorway. Heavy goods vehicles, coaches etc. are obvious examples. The list includes motor vehicles towing trailers.

A MOTORIST whose car was fitted with a tow-bar hired a trailer for the day in order to move some heavy furniture. Evidently unfamiliar with the Highway Code and blissfully unaware that his vehicle was not allowed in the third lane and that the speed limit for the vehicle was 60 m.p.h., he proceeded to drive in the third lane at speeds approaching 100 m.p.h. Stopped by the police, he received a summons alleging that he drove an unauthorised vehicle in the third lane and that he exceeded the speed limit for the class of vehicle.

He pleaded guilty to both charges, was fined £50 for the first offence, licence endorsed with 3 penalty points, and for the speeding offence he was fined £200 and disqualified from driving for 56 days.

Defences

1. That you used the third lane in an emergency or in order to avoid an accident.

2. That you used the third lane in order to overtake a wide load and that you returned to one of the other lanes as soon as it was practicable to do so.

DRIVING IN CONTRAVENTION OF A TRAFFIC SIGN

On [date] at [place] you did drive a motor vehicle namely . . . in contravention of the indication given by a traffic sign namely . . .

Contrary to section 17(4) of the Road Traffic Regulation Act, 1984.

Maximum Penalty

Level 4 fine

Licence endorsed with 3 penalty points

Disqualification at the discretion of the court.

This statute covers, for example, driving on a slip road against no entry signs and driving beyond flashing red stop lights.

Alcohol-related Offences

The most common offences are:

1. failing to provide a roadside breath test;
2. driving/attempting to drive with excess alcohol;
3. being in charge of a vehicle with excess alcohol;
4. after driving/attempting to drive, refusing to provide samples for analysis;
5. after being in charge of a vehicle, failing to provide samples for analysis.

The law sets out proper procedures for dealing with the motorist at the roadside and at the police station. The majority of successful defences to a charge rely on some error in procedure.

THE PROCEDURES

At the Roadside

A person driving, attempting to drive, or **in charge of** a motor vehicle on a road or in a public place may be required to provide a breath test.

> *Key Terms*
>
> ■ **In charge of** A person whose actions fall short of driving but who is shown to be in control of a vehicle

The vehicle must be a vehicle intended for or adapted for road use. A breath test may be required not only on a road but in any place to which the public have access, including, for example, the car park of a public house, the forecourt of a filling station or a building site.

The request for a breath test may only be made by a police officer in uniform. In requesting the test, there is no particular form of words but the officer must make it clear that a breath test is required. The test must be conducted 'at or near a place where the requirement to provide such a test is made'.

A police officer may only request a roadside breath test in the following circumstances:

1. if the officer has reasonable cause to suspect that you have committed or are committing a moving traffic offence;

2. if, having stopped a vehicle for any reason, the officer has reasonable cause to suspect that the person driving/attempting to drive/in charge of the vehicle has consumed alcohol;

3. if the officer has reasonable cause to believe that you were the person driving/attempting to drive/in charge of a vehicle which was involved in an accident.

The question is not whether or not you have actually committed an offence, or whether or not you have actually consumed alcohol. It is sufficient that the police officer has reasonable cause to suspect either of these. In practice, a breath test is seldom required on suspicion of a moving traffic offence, but when suspicion of consumption of alcohol arises.

After an accident, it is not sufficient that the police officer has reasonable cause to suspect, the officer must have reasonable cause to believe. This is only a matter of degree but belief has to be more definite than mere suspicion.

Random Breath Tests

There is much confusion about random breath tests. A police officer is entitled to stop any vehicle, but an officer cannot stop any vehicle which happens to come along and require the driver to provide a breath test. The officer can, however, stop any vehicle which happens to come along and, if there is reason to suspect that the driver has consumed alcohol, then the officer may require the driver to provide a breath test.

The difference is the suspicion which must arise between the stopping and the request for a breath test.

Breath Tests Other Than at the Roadside

A person who was driving/attempting to drive or in charge of a vehicle involved in an accident, who is injured and taken to hospital, may be required to provide a breath test at the hospital or at a police station specified by the police officer.

A person whom a police officer has reasonable cause to believe was driving/attempting to drive or in charge of a vehicle involved in an accident in which injury to a person was caused, and who subsequently leaves the scene of the accident, is required to allow a police officer to enter their home for the purpose of providing a breath test.

After a Roadside Breath Test, What Happens Next?

If you provide a positive roadside sample, or if you refuse or fail to provide a sample, you will be arrested, conveyed to a police station and required to provide two samples of breath for analysis.

The Arrest and Caution

This is a positive act by the police officer who will usually use a set form of words to tell you that you are being arrested. The present form is:

I am arresting you for failing to provide a specimen of breath/roadside breath test without reasonable excuse. You are not obliged to say anything but anything you say will be taken down and used in evidence.

The police officer must make it clear:

1. that you are being arrested;

2. why you are being arrested;

3. what your rights are upon arrest.

If there is any major deviation from the above, the arrest is unlawful and anything that follows that unlawful arrest is not admissible in a court of law.

At the Police Station

You will be required to provide two samples of breath for analysis by an approved automatic measuring device, a Lion Intoximeter or a Camic Breath Analyser. If the print-out gives different readings, the police will rely on the lower reading. If you fail to provide samples of breath without reasonable excuse, you commit an offence.

A MOTORIST was known by the police to be a heavy drinker and had two convictions for driving with excess alcohol. He was observed at 11 o'clock one evening driving erratically, was stopped and a roadside breath test was requested. He refused to take the test, was arrested and conveyed to a police station.

Unknown to the police, they had stopped him on possibly the only evening in the last decade when he had consumed no alcohol at all. Highly indignant and protesting his innocence, he refused to provide samples for analysis and was charged with that offence. Coming to his senses within half an hour, he agreed to provide a breath sample so that he might be permitted to drive home. The test confirmed that he had not consumed alcohol.

He appeared in court and, having taken legal advice, pleaded guilty to refusing to provide samples for analysis. He was given a conditional discharge but was, nevertheless, disqualified from driving for 12 months.

If you refuse to provide samples of breath because you are unfit, out of condition and breathless, that is not reasonable excuse. If, on the other hand, you suffer from a chronic breathing problem (such as asthma) and would be unable to provide the volume of breath necessary, that is a reasonable excuse. If you have an inhaler or other medication with you, show it to the police officer. Give him the name of your doctor.

A great many defendants use the excuse that they 'tried their hardest', but were unable to provide the required volume of breath. That is not a reasonable excuse. Neither is it a reasonable excuse that your failure to provide was because you were so drunk or under such stress that you were physically incapable of providing the samples.

In a recent case, however, the defendant's state of shock was found to be a reasonable excuse.

A DRIVER gave one sample of breath but then lost her composure and was unable to provide a second sample. She was clearly distraught and sobbing continuously. At the magistrates' court she was found to have reasonable excuse. The Crown Prosecution Service appealed to the High Court. Dismissing the appeal, the judge commented that the defendant's state of shock was a substantial factor in her inability to provide a specimen.

Blood or urine samples may be requested instead of breath in one of the following circumstances:

1. at the time specimens are requested no automatic measuring device is available or is not in proper working order;

2. the offence is one involving drugs and the police officer has taken medical advice that your condition may be due to drugs;

3. the police officer making the request has reasonable cause to believe that breath samples should not be required for health reasons.

Again, you may not refuse to provide samples without a reasonable excuse. A haemophiliac would have a reasonable excuse for not providing blood. Refusing to give a sample of blood because you fear the sight of blood or needles is not a reasonable excuse. Neither is it a reasonable excuse that you cannot provide a sample of urine because you have 'just been'. A person who has a medical condition which makes it difficult to pass water may have a reasonable excuse.

If, having provided positive samples of breath, the lower reading is 50 micrograms per litre of breath or less, you must be offered the option of providing a specimen of blood or urine. You will be asked which option you prefer, but you cannot insist on one or the other. After hearing what you have to say, the police officer will decide which sample you should provide. Blood may not be taken without your consent, but if you refuse that consent unreasonably, the police will rely on the breath test reading.

If urine samples are requested, you will be required to provide two samples within an hour. Blood samples will be taken by a police surgeon. An extraordinary number of motorists who have provided a sample of breath and are offered the option of providing a blood or urine sample fail to take advantage of that option. If the police officer gives you the option of providing a blood sample, there is a chance that you could be below the limit by the time a police surgeon arrives.

The samples will be divided and you may take one away for independent analysis. You should take advantage of this. Be very careful that you store the sample in accordance with the instructions which you will have been given at the police station. Incorrect storage will destroy any chance you may have of a successful defence.

Independent analysis is conducted by a forensic chemist. Your solicitor will arrange this for you. A defence based on a significant difference in the results of analysis should be presented by a solicitor or barrister. The forensic chemist will give evidence in court. You will be responsible for all fees and costs, and they could be very substantial.

If you are to be charged, you will be cautioned. Anything you say may be written down and may be used in evidence against you, so be very careful what you say. You will be asked to sign the charge sheet and, usually, you will be given bail with a duty to surrender to a magistrates' court at an early date. You will not, of course, be permitted to drive home until the police are confident that you are fit to do so, but you may be released earlier if someone comes to fetch you.

If you are not given bail, you will be kept in police cells. Be sure that you ask to see a solicitor.

THE OFFENCES

Failing to Provide a Roadside Breath Test

A motorist suspected of committing or having committed a moving traffic offence:

That you on [date] at [place] being a person driving a motor vehicle or being a person attempting to drive a motor vehicle having been required to provide a specimen of breath for a breath test by a constable in uniform (who had reasonable cause to suspect you of having committed a traffic offence while the said vehicle was in motion/after having committed a traffic offence while the said vehicle was in motion) did without reasonable excuse fail to do so.

Contrary to section 6(4) of the Road Traffic Act, 1988.

A motorist suspected of having consumed alcohol:

That you on [date] at [place] being a person driving a motor vehicle or being a person attempting to drive a motor vehicle having been required to provide a specimen of breath for a breath test by a constable in uniform who had reasonable cause to suspect that you have alcohol in your body did without reasonable excuse fail to do so.

Contrary to section 6(4) of the Road Traffic Act, 1988.

A motorist involved in an accident:

That you on [date] at [place] being a person whom a constable in uniform had reasonable cause (a) to believe was driving a motor vehicle at the time (b) to believe was attempting to drive a motor vehicle at the time (one only) when an accident occurred owing to the presence of that vehicle (a) on a road or (b) in a public place having been required by the said constable did without reasonable excuse fail to provide a specimen of breath for a breath test.

Contrary to section 6(4) of the Road Traffic Act, 1988.

Maximum penalty

Level 3 fine

Driving licence endorsed with 4 penalty points

Endorsement Code DR70

Disqualification at the discretion of the court.

See **special reasons** for not endorsing (Chapter 1).

No **fixed penalty** available.

No facility to plead **guilty in absence**.

The offence is committed either if you refuse to take the breath test or if you fail without reasonable excuse to provide the required volume of breath. You may, for example, have blown into the bag but failed to inflate it sufficiently.

If you suffer from a chronic respiratory problem and are unable to provide the volume of breath necessary, that is a **reasonable excuse**. Shock and stress rendering you incapable of inflating the bag sufficiently may amount to a **reasonable excuse**.

It is not a reasonable excuse that you have not consumed alcohol, that you have not committed/were not committing a moving traffic offence or that you were not the driver of the vehicle involved in an accident.

A MOTORIST had driven 25 miles to visit some friends. Returning home in the early hours of the morning, he had driven to within a few miles of his home when he felt too tired to drive any further. He parked his car on a grass verge beside the road and fell asleep. He was awakened by a police officer knocking on the window of

---

Key Terms

■ **Special reasons** Reasons special to the circumstances of the offence which allow a court a discretion not to endorse or not to disqualify ■ **Fixed penalty** Provides an opportunity to have the matter dealt with other than by a court ■ **Guilty in absence** A guilty plea by post or otherwise in the absence of the defendant ■ **Reasonable excuse** A genuine excuse, e.g. a chronic respiratory problem

his car. He wound the window down and, when asked if he had been drinking, replied 'no' – and promptly wound the window back up again.

Thereafter, no further knocking on the window could persuade the motorist to allow the officer access. This unreasonable behaviour aroused the officer's suspicion and he called for assistance. He and a colleague gained access to the car by breaking a rear window. The indignant motorist refused to take a breath test. He was arrested and conveyed to a police station where he agreed to provide samples for analysis. The test was negative.

The motorist was charged and convicted of failing to provide a roadside breath test. He was fined £120, had to pay £30 prosecution costs and his licence was endorsed with 4 penalty points.

If the breath test is required following an accident, the prosecution must prove that there was an accident and that you were the person driving/attempting to drive or in charge of a vehicle involved in that accident.

Defences

See pages 123, 124 and 137.

Driving/Attempting to Drive with Excess Alcohol

On [date] at [place] you did drive/attempt to drive a motor vehicle on road (or did drive/attempt to drive a motor vehicle in a public place) having consumed alcohol in such a quantity that the proportion thereof in your blood/breath/urine (one only) exceeded the prescribed limit.

Contrary to section 5(1)(a) of the Road Traffic Act, 1988.

Maximum penalty

Level 5 fine and/or imprisonment for up to 6 months.

Mandatory disqualification from driving for at least 12 months for a first offence, at least 3 years for a second or subsequent offence

Endorsement Code DR10.

No **fixed penalty** available

No facility to plead guilty in absence.

If **special reasons** for not disqualifying, licence endorsed with 3–11 penalty points.

There is an offence of **aiding and abetting** the commission of the above offence for which the penalties are similar, but for which disqualification from driving is not obligatory. Endorsement Code DR10.

Note that 12 months is the minimum period of disqualification on conviction for a first offence. In practice, magistrates are provided with guidelines including a graph from which they read off the alcohol content and the recommended period of disqualification. Thus disqualification for periods of, say, 15 months etc. are not uncommon.

In addition to disqualification from driving, the most likely penalty is a fine. Imprisonment becomes a real possi-

---

Key Terms

■ **Fixed penalty** Provides an opportunity to have the matter dealt with other than by a court ■ **Special reasons** Reasons special to the circumstances of the offence which allow a court a discretion not to endorse or not to disqualify ■ **Aiding and abetting** Helping another to commit an offence

bility upon conviction for a second offence within a ten-year period and even for a first offence where the alcohol content is shown to be three times the legal limit. A probation order with a condition that you attend a prescribed Alcohol Offenders Course is a common sentence. A community service order or a combination order are other possibilities.

You will either have provided a positive roadside breath test or failed to provide such a test. You must have been driving or attempting to drive.

- **Driving**   The prosecution must prove an element of controlling the direction and movement of the vehicle: a motorist steering a vehicle under tow was found to be driving; a motorist pushing a car with one foot inside it was found to be driving; a motorcyclist sitting astride his machine while pushing and steering it was found to be driving even though the ignition was not on.

- **Attempting to drive**   The prosecution must prove an act sufficiently close to driving. Generally the difference will depend on whether or not the vehicle is in motion: a motorist who attempted to start his vehicle by putting the wrong key in the ignition was found to be attempting to drive; a motorist who attempted to start a vehicle which could not possibly start because of a mechanical defect was attempting to drive.

Evidence of excess alcohol must be established. In the case of breath, this is provided by a certificate accompanied by a print-out. Blood and urine samples are analysed by an 'authorised analyst' who will provide a certificate of analysis. Where some time elapsed between driving ceasing and the provision of specimens for analysis, back calculations may be applied.

Depending on the rate at which alcohol is consumed, its level will continue to rise for a short time and then it will fall. The rate of fall will depend on many factors including

Back calculations

Back calculation arises when a motorist consumes alcohol between the time of ceasing to drive and the time of providing a breath test or samples for analysis. The defence will argue that it is this post-consumption of alcohol which produces a reading above the limit, that the alcohol you consumed before ceasing to drive would not have been sufficient to produce a reading above the legal limit at that time.

This is, very definitely, the province of an expert. Expert witnesses will give evidence for the defence and for the prosecution. The defence will present calculations to demonstrate that, had it not been for the post-consumption, you would have been below the legal limit. The expert witness for the prosecution will attempt to show that this is not the case.

The circumstances in which the post-consumption of alcohol occurred will be relevant. You may have had no reason to believe that you would be required to provide a breath test. You may have consumed alcohol because you were feeling ill or were in a state of shock. You should know, however, that if you deliberately consume alcohol after driving and before you are breathalysed in order to confuse the issue, you may be charged with attempting to pervert the course of justice . . .

whether wine, spirits or beer were consumed, how quickly it was consumed, whether it was consumed on an empty stomach or with/after a meal. The rate of absorption of alcohol in the body also depends on the sex and physical characteristics of the defendant.

Where a defendant consumed alcohol, drove a vehicle and consumed more after ceasing to drive, but before providing samples for analysis, back calculation will again apply.

If you wish to contest the findings of the authorised analyst, it is essential that you have your portion of the sample analysed independently and that your analyst gives conflicting expert evidence in court.

Defences

See page 137.

Being in Charge of a Vehicle with Excess Alcohol

On [date] at [place] you were in charge of a motor vehicle on a road or other public place after consuming alcohol in such a quantity that the proportion thereof in your blood/breath/urine exceeded the prescribed limit.

Contrary to section 5 of the Road Traffic Act, 1988.

Maximum penalty

Level 4 fine and/or 3 months' imprisonment

Licence endorsed with 10 penalty points

Endorsement Code DR40

Disqualification at the discretion of the court.

See **special reasons** for not endorsing.

No fixed penalty available

Key Terms

■ **Special reasons** Reasons special to the circumstances of the offence which allow a court a discretion not to endorse or not to disqualify

No facility for pleading guilty in absence.

Again, there must have been a positive roadside breath test or a failure to take such a test and the prosecution must prove excess alcohol as in driving with excess alcohol (see page 130).

The words 'in charge' imply very much a matter of fact and degree. The owner or keeper of a vehicle, or any person who has recently driven a vehicle, may remain in charge of that vehicle.

AN ACCIDENT in which a person was injured was caused because a vehicle had been parked in a dangerous position. The person who had parked the vehicle half an hour previously was required to provide a roadside breath test. When this proved positive, he was arrested and, after providing samples of breath for analysis, he was charged with being in charge of the vehicle with excess alcohol.

Any person sitting in a vehicle or even being near a vehicle who might imminently take control of that vehicle may be in charge of that vehicle.

A MOTORIST spent two hours in a public house and, realising that he was unfit to drive through the quantity of alcohol he had consumed, handed the ignition key of his car to the landlord. At closing time, a police officer observed the motorist asleep in the passenger seat of the car. A breath test was requested and proved positive. When, however, it was discovered that the motorist did not possess a key to the ignition, and that he had no intention imminently to take control of the vehicle, no charge was brought.

Where there is an intention to continue to drive, courts have found that the motorist is not in charge but actually driving the vehicle. A motorist who was changing a wheel and a motorist who got out of his car to buy a newspaper were found to be driving their vehicles.

Where there is any doubt about continuing to drive, the relevant questions are as follows:

1. What was the purpose of the stop?

2. For how long was the vehicle stopped?

3. Did the driver get out of the vehicle?

4. Are you at the end of your journey?

If a motorist is charged with driving with excess alcohol in these circumstances, the defence must dispute the continuing to drive element. If the vehicle was stopped for a long time or if the driver had reached the end of the journey, continuing to drive is difficult to establish and the correct charge is one of being in charge of a vehicle.

Defences

See page 137.

After Driving/Attempting to Drive, Refusing to Provide Samples for Analysis

On [date] at [place] having been required by a police constable to provide two specimens for analysis (or a specimen of blood or urine for a laboratory test) you failed, without reasonable excuse to do so.

Contrary to section 7 of the Road Traffic Act, 1988.

Maximum penalty

Level 5 fine and/or 6 months' imprisonment.

Mandatory disqualification for 12 months for a first offence or for 3 years for a second or subsequent offence committed within a 10-year period.

Endorsement Code DR30.

See **special reasons.**

No **fixed penalty** available.

No facility to plead guilty in absence.

In practice, the court may well take the view that refusal to provide specimens represents an attempt to evade the consequences of a particularly high alcohol content. The period of disqualification is likely to be 18 months or more.

The prosecution must prove driving/attempting to drive as above. There must have been a positive roadside breath test or a failure to provide and the prosecution must prove that you refused or failed without reasonable excuse to provide samples for analysis.

For what may constitute **reasonable excuse,** see pages 123–4.

Defences

See page 137.

Key Terms

■ **Special reasons** Reasons special to the circumstances of the offence which allow a court a discretion not to endorse or not to disqualify ■ **Fixed penalty** Provides an opportunity to have the matter dealt with other than by a court ■ **Reasonable excuse** A genuine excuse, e.g. a chronic respiratory problem

After Being in Charge of a Vehicle, Failed to Provide Specimens for Analysis

On [date] at [place] having been required by a police constable to provide two specimens of breath for analysis (or a specimen of blood or urine for a laboratory test) you failed without reasonable excuse to do so.

Contrary to section 7 of the Road Traffic Act, 1988.

Maximum penalty

Level 4 fine and/or 3 months' imprisonment.

Licence endorsed with 10 penalty points.

Endorsement Code DR60.

Disqualification at the discretion of the court.

See **special reasons** for not endorsing.

No **fixed penalty** available.

No facility to plead guilty in absence.

The prosecution must prove being in charge as above. There must have been a positive roadside breath test or a failure to provide and the prosecution must prove that you refused or failed without reasonable excuse to provide samples for analysis.

For **reasonable excuse,** see page 127.

DEFENCES

The following represent defences to all charges.

1. Mistaken identity: it wasn't you, you weren't there.
2. The vehicle was not a motor vehicle.
3. The alleged offence was not committed on a road or in a public place.
4. You were not driving, attempting to drive or in charge of the vehicle.
5. There was an error in procedure at the roadside:
   (a) the police officer was not in uniform;
   (b) the police officer did not have reasonable cause to suspect that you had committed a moving traffic offence or did not have reasonable cause to suspect that you had consumed alcohol;
   (c) the requirement to provide a breath test was not made clear or was not understood;
   (d) the consequences of failing to provide a roadside breath test were not made clear;
   (e) you had a reasonable excuse for not providing a roadside breath test;
   (f) the breath test was not carried out at or near the place where the request was made.

And, when the breath test was required after an accident:

   (g) there was no accident;
   (h) the police officer did not have reasonable cause to believe that you were the person driving, attempting to drive or in charge of a vehicle involved in an accident;
   (i) a breath test was required at a hospital despite the objection of the attending physician;
   (j) the police officer was trespassing, for example, a

police officer has reason to believe that the house-holder was the driver of a vehicle involved in an accident and enters the house against the will of the householder, but no personal injury was sustained in the accident.

It is a defence to any subsequent charge if:
(k) the arrest was illegal;
(l) no caution was given or the caution was not understood.

It is a defence to any subsequent charge if there was an error in procedure at the police station:
(a) the intoximeter was faulty;
(b) the consequences of refusing to provide specimens were not explained to you or not understood by you;
(c) the police officer took no notice of a valid reason for not providing a sample;
(d) after providing two samples of breath, the lower reading was 50 mcg of alcohol per litre or less and you were not given the option of providing samples of blood or urine;
(e) the subsequent arrest was illegal;
(f) the charge was defective, e.g. no caution was given or the caution was not understood.

A MOTORIST provided two samples of breath for analysis. The lower reading was 48 mcg of alcohol per litre of breath. He was not offered the option of providing specimens of blood or urine, was charged and released on bail. When the error in procedure became apparent, the charge was withdrawn.

Specific Defences

It is a defence to failing to provide specimens for analysis if you had a reasonable excuse.

It is a defence to any charge involving driving if you show that you were neither driving nor attempting to drive. It is a defence to the being in charge offences if you show that you were not in charge.

Post-consumption of alcohol (or drinking after you have ceased to drive the vehicle or ceased to be in charge of the vehicle) is a defence to driving with excess alcohol or to being in charge with excess alcohol, provided you can prove:

1. that such post-consumption occurred; and

2. that the post-consumption was the sole cause of the excess alcohol.

A significant difference in the results of analysis of samples of blood or urine is a defence to driving with excess alcohol or being in charge with excess alcohol.

Special Reasons for Not Disqualifying

If you consume an alcoholic drink which is stronger than you believe because it has been 'laced' by some third party, you may have **special reasons**. You must prove that you were not aware and could not have been aware of what you were drinking and that the alcohol added to your drink was responsible for the excess alcohol. Back calculation is relevant and expert evidence is essential. Your solicitor will advise you and make arrangements for a qualified chemist to give such expert evidence on your behalf.

Key Terms

■ **Special reasons** Reasons special to the circumstances of the offence which allow a court a discretion not to endorse or not to disqualify

A motorist who has consumed alcohol and has no intention of driving, but does so in a real emergency, may have
special reasons. You must prove that there was no
way of dealing with the emergency other than to drive and
that you ceased to drive once the emergency was over.

A motorist who moves a car a short distance may have
special reasons. The definition of 'a short distance' will
depend on the circumstances of each particular case. A
motorist who drives a matter of yards, say from the road into
the driveway of a house, may have **special reasons**.

A TREE was blown down in a gale and a police
officer knocked on the door of a house and asked
the occupant to move his car. The motorist did as
requested and was involved in conversation with
the police officer when the latter had reason to suspect that
the motorist had consumed alcohol. A roadside breath test
proved positive, the motorist was arrested and, after providing samples for analysis, was charged with driving with
excess alcohol.

He pleaded guilty but the court found special reasons for
not disqualifying.

What You Should Do

At the roadside

If you provide a positive breath test or if you refuse to provide a breath test (and this includes not inflating the bag sufficiently), you will be arrested and conveyed to a police
station.

If you suffer from some medical condition which pre-
vents you from providing sufficient volume of breath to
inflate the bag fully, you should make this clear to the
police officer. You may not be charged with failing to pro-

vide a breath test. If you are charged, you may have a defence.

At the police station

The initial request will be for two samples of breath. If you have a good reason for being unable to provide the required volume, make it clear to the police officer. Show the officer an inhaler or any other medication you may have for a breathing problem. Give the officer the name of your doctor.

Make it clear that you have a good reason for refusing.

If, having provided two samples of breath, the lower reading is 50 mcg or less, always take advantage of the option of providing blood or urine.

Always take your portion of a blood or urine sample away with you. Samples have a limited life so store them as recommended. If independent analysis of your sample shows an alcohol content different from that alleged by the prosecution, you may have a defence.

After you have been charged

If you believe you may have a defence to a charge, consult a solicitor immediately. If your defence depends on an independent analysis of a sample, that will be arranged for you and, if you subsequently plead not guilty, the solicitor will arrange for an expert witness to give evidence in court.

If you believe you may have **special reasons** for not being disqualified from driving, these are best argued by a solicitor. Consult a solicitor or see the **duty solicitor** when you attend court.

If you believe that imprisonment is a possibility, consult a solicitor. You may qualify for **legal aid**.

If the charge is that of refusing to provide samples for

analysis, the court is likely to take a serious view and you should consider consulting a solicitor or seeing the duty solicitor on the day of your court appearance.

While disqualification from driving is obligatory on conviction for driving with excess alcohol and for after driving, failing to provide samples for analysis, the court is not obliged to disqualify for the '**in charge**' offences. If you are convicted of one of the in charge offences, you may have a better chance of avoiding disqualification if you are represented by a solicitor.

If you intend to plead guilty to a first offence of driving with excess alcohol and analysis revealed no more than a moderate alcohol content, there may be little a solicitor can say that you cannot say for yourself.

If you are unemployed or in receipt of a low income, be sure that you complete a **means form** or tell the magistrates. If you do not, you are likely to be fined more than you can afford to pay. The magistrates will have a period of disqualification in mind based on the level of alcohol. Try to persuade them to impose as short a period as possible. Explain how you came to be drinking and driving. If, despite

---

Key Terms

■ **Duty solicitor** A solicitor available to give advice without charge to defendants in court ■ **Legal aid** Legal representation either free of charge or upon payment of a small contribution ■ **In charge of** A person whose actions fall short of driving but who is shown to be in control of a vehicle ■ **Means form** A document accompanying the summons

drinking and driving, you drove safely, were not involved in an accident and did not commit any other offence, be sure the court is aware of that. Tell the magistrates what effect a long period of disqualification would have on your employment or your ability to find work.

Either Way and Indictable Offences

The following offences may be tried either before a magistrates' court or before a judge and jury at a Crown Court:

1. aggravated vehicle taking;

2. causing danger to road users;

3. dangerous driving;

4. fraudulent use of an **excise licence**.

Except for the last of the above, these are very serious charges and you should definitely consult a solicitor, who will advise you whether you should choose to have the matter dealt with by a Crown Court or whether, given the opportunity, you should have the matter dealt with by a magistrates' court.

If you intend to plead guilty, there is little point in going to a Crown Court. You may well have to wait some weeks, even months, before you are sentenced. You will certainly have to pay a greater sum in costs and you risk a more severe sentence.

Key Terms

■ **Excise licence** A tax disc

If, on the other hand, you intend to plead not guilty, you may believe that you will have a better chance of acquittal by a jury and elect trial before a Crown Court. That is for you to decide but you should bear the following in mind:

1. your case will almost certainly be heard at a much earlier date before a magistrates' court;

2. if, at the preliminary hearing before a magistrates' court, the magistrates announce that they believe the matter is suitable for **summary trial** (i.e. suitable for trial before a magistrates' court), but you, nevertheless, exercise your right to be tried at a Crown Court before a judge and jury, and are found guilty, again you risk a more severe sentence and you will have to pay substantially greater costs.

MODE OF TRIAL PROCEDURE FOR EITHER WAY OFFENCES

Before the magistrates' court, the prosecutor will outline the facts of the case and say whether the prosecution believes that the matter is suitable for trial before a magistrates' court or before a Crown Court. The views of your solicitor will then be given to the court on where your case should be heard.

Key Terms

■ **Either way offence** An offence which may be tried either by a magistrates' court or before a judge and jury at a Crown Court

If the prosecution and the defence both say that the matter is suitable for **summary trial**, the magistrates will usually agree – but they are not obliged to agree. The decision is theirs. They may still order you to be committed to a Crown Court.

If the magistrates consent to summary trial, you will be asked where you wish the matter to be dealt with. Before you decide, you will be told that even if you wish the matter to be dealt with by a magistrates' court there remain circumstances in which you may still be sent to a Crown Court to be sentenced:

1. if it subsequently becomes apparent that the case is more serious than was at first believed; or

2. if you plead guilty or, after a trial, are found guilty and the court then hears information about your character and/or about any previous convictions, which causes the magistrates to believe that their powers of sentence are insufficient.

You should now say where you wish the matter to be dealt with. If you wish the matter to be dealt with by a magistrates' court, you will be asked whether you plead guilty or not guilty and the matter will proceed as described in Chapters 9 and 10. If you choose Crown Court trial, the magistrates have no choice: they must commit you to a Crown Court for trial.

Committal to a Crown Court for Trial

Usually, this is a short hearing before a magistrates' court, known as a paper committal. The purpose is to satisfy the magistrates that there is sufficient evidence to send to a Crown Court. Documents are checked and orders for the attendance of witnesses at the Crown Court will be made. If you are receiving **legal aid**, your solicitor will apply to have this extended to pay for the services of a solicitor and a barrister at the Crown Court.

Reporting restrictions

Unless the court makes an order to the contrary, no details of the proceedings may appear in the press, other than your name, the nature of the charge or charges and the fact that you have been committed to a Crown Court.

Alibi warning

When you are committed, you will be told that, at the Crown Court, you will not be permitted to give evidence of an alibi or to call witnesses in support of an alibi, unless you give details to the court before committal or to the prosecution within seven days. Such details will be thoroughly checked by the police before your trial.

Bail

Finally, the magistrates will decide whether you should be sent to the Crown Court in **custody** or whether you should be given **bail**.

Key Terms

■ **Legal aid** Legal representation either free of charge or upon payment of a small contribution ■ **Custody** A period of detention either in police cells or remand prison ■ **Bail** Release from custody with a duty to surrender to a court at a later date

Committal for Sentence

It is likely that you are being committed for sentence by a judge because the magistrates believe either that you should be sentenced to longer imprisonment than they have the power to impose, or that you should pay a fine and/or compensation greater than they have the power to order.

If the reason for committal is the former, you are likely to be sent to the Crown Court in custody. An application to the magistrates for bail is unlikely to succeed. If bail is refused, your solicitor may apply for bail to a judge in chambers. Such an application is usually heard within 24 hours of the magistrates' court hearing. If that, too, fails, you will remain in custody until you are brought before the Crown Court.

THE OFFENCES

Aggravated Vehicle Taking

1. On [date] at [place] without having the consent of the owner or other lawful authority you took a mechanically propelled vehicle namely ... for your own or another's use.

or On [date] at [place] knowing that a mechanically propelled vehicle namely ... had been taken without the consent of the owner or other lawful authority you drove it/allowed yourself to be carried in or on it.

and

2. after the vehicle was unlawfully taken and before it was recovered
   (a) the vehicle was driven dangerously on a road or other public place
   (b) that, owing to the driving of the vehicle, an accident

occurred whereby injury was caused to any person
(c) that, owing to the driving of the vehicle, an accident
occurred whereby damage was caused to any property,
other than vehicle
(d) that damage was caused to the vehicle.

Contrary to section 12A of the Theft Act, 1968.

Maximum penalty

Before a magistrates' court

Level 5 fine and/or 6 months' imprisonment.

Obligatory disqualification from driving for a minimum of 12 months.

No **fixed penalty** available.

No facility to plead guilty in absence.

Compensation may be ordered.

If **special reasons** apply, licence endorsed with 3–11 penalty points

Endorsement Code UT50.

This is an either way offence except where the only aggravating element is damage to the vehicle and/or property, and the value of such damage does not exceed the sum of £2000 (1994). In these circumstances only, the matter may be heard before a magistrates' court.

Key Terms

■ **Fixed penalty** Provides an opportunity to have the matter dealt with other than by a court ■ **Special reasons** Reasons special to the circumstances of the offence which allow a court a discretion not to endorse or not to disqualify

Before a Crown Court

Unlimited fine and/or 2 years' imprisonment

(Where aggravation relates to an injury caused to any person and the accident causes the person's death, the maximum term of imprisonment is increased to 5 years.)

Obligatory disqualification.

Compensation may be ordered.

Special reasons may apply.

The court will take a more serious view in the following circumstances:

1. the offence was committed while on bail;

2. an attempt was made to avoid detection or arrest;

3. where there is evidence of drink or drugs;

4. where it is shown that the theft was planned.

The court will also consider the overall culpability of the driving, what distance was travelled and over what length of time. Were excessive speeds reached? Was injury or severe damage caused, or was there a serious risk of such injury or damage?

Since the offence is committed primarily by young offenders, the fact that the defendant is a young person will not be regarded as an extenuating circumstance.

Taking a Vehicle Without Consent

All the essential elements of the 'basic' offence, i.e. taking a vehicle without consent or being carried in a vehicle taken without consent, must be established and, after the unlawful taking but before the vehicle was recovered, one of the aggravating elements described in the statute occurred.

Note that the statute refers to a mechanically propelled vehicle, not simply a motor vehicle. The prosecution must prove beyond reasonable doubt (a) the basic offence and (b) one or more of the aggravating features described in the statute. It is sufficient to show that the aggravating feature was present. It is not necessary to prove that the defendant was responsible, for example, the vehicle was driven dangerously, not that the defendant drove the vehicle dangerously.

Defences

1. Mistaken identity: it wasn't me, I wasn't there.
2. All the defences that apply to the basic offence.
3. The driving, accident, injury or damage occurred before the basic offence was committed.
4. The defendant was neither in or on the vehicle nor in its immediate vicinity when the driving, accident, injury or damage took place.

Special reasons for not disqualifying

It is not a **special reason** that the defendant was not driving. The driver and any passengers are equally culpable.

Alternative verdict

When the evidence does not support a conviction for aggravated vehicle taking, the defendant may be convicted of taking a vehicle without consent or of being carried in a vehicle taken without consent.

Key Terms

■ **Special reasons** Reasons special to the circumstances of the offence which allow a court a discretion not to endorse or not to disqualify

What you should do

Charged with this offence, you are likely to be kept in police custody for some time. Be sure to ask to see a solicitor.

Causing Danger to Road Users

On [date] at [place] without lawful authority or reasonable cause you knowingly (1) caused [identify article] to be on or over a road (2) interfered with a motor vehicle (trailer or cycle) namely . . . (3) interfered (directly or indirectly) with traffic equipment, namely . . . in such circumstances that it would be obvious to a reasonable person that to do so would be dangerous.

Contrary to section 22A of the Road Traffic Act, 1991.

Maximum penalty

Before a magistrates' court

Level 5 fine and/or 6 months' imprisonment.

Compensation may be ordered.

No **fixed penalty** available.

No facility to plead guilty in absence.

Before a Crown Court

Unlimited fine and/or 7 years' imprisonment.

Compensation may be ordered.

Key Terms

■ **Fixed penalty** Provides an opportunity to have the matter dealt with other than by a court

The offence

A person who knowingly, i.e. deliberately, commits an act in such circumstances that it would be obvious to a reasonable person that it would be dangerous to do so, commits an offence.

Danger means danger of injury to a person or of serious damage to property and it is not necessary to show that such injury or damage occurred, only that the act could have led to such injury or damage.

Interference may be to a motor vehicle, trailer or cycle and to traffic equipment – anything lawfully placed on or near a road, a road sign, fence, barrier, traffic light etc.

Defences

1. You did not commit the act alleged.

2. The act was not committed deliberately.

3. It would not have been obvious to a reasonable person that danger would have been caused.

4. The 'traffic equipment' with which you interfered was not capable of being described as traffic equipment or was placed there unlawfully.

What you should do

Consult a solicitor.

Dangerous Driving

On [date] at [place] you drove a mechanically propelled vehicle namely . . . dangerously on a road/public place namely. . .

Contrary to section 2 of the Road Traffic Act, 1988 and Schedule 2 of the Road Traffic Act, 1988.

Maximum penalties

Before a magistrates' court

6 months' imprisonment and/or fine Level 5.

12 months' disqualification compulsory for a first offence.

3 years' disqualification compulsory for a second offence committed within 3 years.

Extended driving test compulsory.

Compensation may be ordered.

No **fixed penalty** available.

No facility to plead guilty in absence.

Where **special reasons** are found, licence endorsed with 10 penalty points for a first offence or with 3–11 points for a second offence within 3 years.

Endorsement Code DD40.

Before a Crown Court

Unlimited fine and/or 2 years' imprisonment.

Compensation may be ordered.

Obligatory disqualification.

Extended driving test compulsory.

Key Terms

■ **Fixed penalty** Provides an opportunity to have the matter dealt with other than by a court ■ **Special reasons** Reasons special to the circumstances of the offence which allow a court a discretion not to endorse or not to disqualify ■ **Guilty in absence** A guilty plea by post or otherwise in the absence of the defendant

A motorist convicted of dangerous driving before a magistrates' court is likely to be dealt with by way a community penalty. There is some risk of a custodial sentence. The court will regard the offence as more serious when:

1. there is any attempt to avoid detection or arrest;

2. there is evidence of drinking or of drugs;

3. there is evidence of excessive speed;

4. there is evidence that warnings (e.g. from passengers) were ignored;

5. the bad driving is deliberate and prolonged;

6. there is evidence of racing or 'showing off'.

'Dangerous' is defined as danger of either injury to any person or of serious damage to property.

The offence may be committed by the driver of any mechanically propelled vehicle, i.e. any such vehicle whether or not it is intended or adapted for road use, e.g. fork-lift truck or dumper truck. The offence may be committed not only on a road but in any public place, i.e. any place to which the public have access, e.g. a building site, car park, forecourt etc.

The offence is committed in the following circumstances:

1. If the manner of your driving falls far below that which would be expected of a competent and careful driver, and that it would be obvious to such a competent and careful driver that it would be dangerous to drive in such a manner. Dangerous driving in these circumstances may include instances of (a) intimidatory driving, (b) tail-gating (driving too close to the vehicle in front to make it give way), (c) selfish driving (e.g. overtaking a long line of traffic and pulling in sharply).

2. If the state of the vehicle you were driving was such that it

would be obvious to a competent and careful driver that to drive a vehicle in such a condition would be dangerous. The state of the vehicle includes anything attached to the vehicle or the way it is attached, carried on or in it, or the way it was carried.

You may be convicted of driving dangerously even if you drove the vehicle faultlessly and competently, and entirely ignorant of any faults, if the faults would have been obvious to a competent and careful driver. If, on the other hand, it is shown that you knew about a fault or defect, it will be assumed that a competent and careful driver, would also have that knowledge.

Defences

Whether the manner of your driving falls far below that which would be expected of a competent and careful driver, or whether a fault or defect would have been obvious to a competent and careful driver, are matters which the magistrates or a jury must decide.

Automatism

A person sitting in the driving seat while the vehicle is in motion is deemed to be the driver, unless it can be shown that the person was temporarily incapable of controlling the vehicle because of being in a coma or suffering from an epileptic fit or being attacked by a swarm of bees etc. Self-induced automatism, e.g. through drink or drugs, is not a defence.

A MOTORIST lost control of his vehicle and collided with a vehicle driving in the opposite direction. Injury and severe damage were caused. Charged with dangerous driving, he pleaded not guilty, claiming that he was temporarily unable to control his vehicle because a wasp had stung him below his eye.

The police evidence was that the drivers of both vehicles were required to provide roadside samples of breath and that, while the defendant was not over the limit, he had been drinking. The defendant was convicted, fined £1000, and disqualified from driving for 12 months and thereafter until he passed a driving test.

Necessity or duress

The driver drove dangerously in order to avoid an imminent threat of death or serious injury; nothing less will suffice. Police officers, firemen, ambulancemen etc. driving in emergencies have no exemption from prosecution for dangerous driving. Such a driver owes the same duty of care to the public as a civilian driver.

Reasonable force to assist in the arrest of offenders

A motorist who, for example, observed a ram-raid and drove into the path of the getaway car to prevent its escape, may have a defence to a charge of dangerous driving.

Alternative verdict

The court has the power to convict on the lesser charge of careless or inconsiderate driving where the evidence does not support a charge of dangerous driving. The court may do so whether or not the prosecution brings the alternative charge.

AN ARMY driving instructor was driving his car on a motorway at 60 m.p.h. in fog. He overtook a slow-moving police car and some miles further on, when the fog had cleared, the police car caused him to stop. He was arrested and charged with dangerous driving. He pleaded not guilty.

Two police officers gave evidence that it was possible to judge visibility from the metre posts beside the motorway and that visibility was no more than 50 m when the defendant overtook them. The defendant gave evidence that he, too, was aware that it was possible to measure distances by referring to the metre posts. He claimed that the fog was thinning and that visibility at the relevant time was 75 m.

The court heard evidence that the road was dry, that the brakes of the defendant's vehicle were in good working order and that the tyres were not worn. The defendant also gave evidence that he had recently passed a test which confirmed exceptionally good eyesight.

The court dismissed the charge of dangerous driving, but found the defendant guilty of driving without due care and attention. He was fined £150, was ordered to pay half the costs of the prosecution and his driving licence was endorsed with 6 penalty points.

What you should do

If you are charged with this offence, you should consult a solicitor. You may qualify for **legal aid**.

Fraudulent Use of an Excise Licence

On [date] at [place] you (forged/fraudulently altered/fraudulently used/fraudulently lent to another/fraudulently allowed to be used by another) a (licence/registration document) under the Vehicles (Excise) Act 1971 namely...

Contrary to section 26(1)(c) of the Vehicles (Excise) Act, 1971.

Key Terms

■ **Legal aid** Legal representation either free of charge or upon payment of a small contribution

Maximum penalty

Before a magistrates' court

Level 5 fine.

Before a Crown Court

Unlimited fine and/or imprisonment for a term not exceeding 2 years.

'To forge'

To make a false mark with the intention that it should be regarded as genuine – an intent to defraud or deceive.

'Fraudulently'

The word 'fraudulently' has a wider meaning not confined to economic loss, and can include deceiving a person in authority into thinking a vehicle is properly taxed. The prosecution must prove an intention to deceive.

The vast majority of offences dealt with by a magistrates' court are committed or are alleged to have been committed by a person who alters the registration mark on a tax disc so that it coincides with that of the vehicle the person is using. It is an offence that is easily detected. Often the make of vehicle shown on the tax disc does not relate to the vehicle and the forgery is evident even on cursory inspection.

There is likely to be a charge of using a vehicle without an **excise licence** and, possibly, a claim for back duty from the DVLA. An additional charge of theft may arise when the tax disc has been taken from a vehicle other than one which is, or was, owned by the defendant.

Key Terms

■ **Excise licence** A tax disc

Defences

1. It wasn't you who altered the tax disc.

2. You had no intention to deceive.

What you should do

If you intend to plead guilty, do so before the magistrates' court. If you intend to plead not guilty, think very carefully before electing to be tried before a Crown Court. Conviction could result in a term of imprisonment. Before a magistrates' court conviction will result in no more than a fine.

The level of the fine will depend on your ability to pay, but the penalty will be more severe than would have been the case if you had used the vehicle with an out-of-date tax disc or, indeed, no tax disc at all.

INDICTABLE OFFENCES

---

1. Causing death by careless driving while unfit through alcohol or drugs.

2. Causing death by dangerous driving.

3. Manslaughter involving a motor vehicle

Clearly very serious allegations, these may only be tried before a judge and jury at a Crown Court. There will be a number of appearances before a magistrates' court before committal. Representation by a solicitor is essential. Your solicitor may make an application for **bail**. **Legal aid** may be granted and your solicitor will apply to have that legal aid extended to afford the services of a barrister or solicitor at the Crown Court.

Key Terms

■ **Bail** Release from custody with a duty to surrender to a court at a later date ■ **Legal aid** Legal representation either free of charge or upon payment of a small contribution

PART III

The Charge and Afterwards

Legal Advice

Charged with an offence, you may wish to consult a solicitor. If you cannot afford to pay, you may qualify for advice given free of charge or at a reduced rate under what is known as the Green Form Scheme. This scheme covers advice given by a solicitor at his or her office only and for up to two hours.

The scheme is rigorously means tested. Those on income support or in receipt of a very low income will receive free advice. Others may be required to make a contribution towards the cost. The solicitor will conduct the means test before any advice is given and you will be required to sign a form agreeing to the means test, and, if you do not qualify for free advice, agreeing to pay part of the cost. The scheme does not extend to representation in court. For that purpose your solicitor may make an application for **legal aid** (and see **duty solicitor** scheme below).

Key Terms

■ **Legal aid** Legal representation either free of charge or upon payment of a small contribution ■ **Duty solicitor** A solicitor available to give advice without charge to defendants in court

LEGAL AID

Legal aid is a scheme whereby a person charged with an offence may be entitled to legal representation by a solicitor or barrister. Such representation may be free (i.e. paid for by the taxpayer) or the person may have to pay part of the cost if he or she has the means to do so.

Entitlement depends on two factors:

1. whether the nature of the offence merits legal representation;

2. whether the defendant's means are such that he or she is entitled to representation either free of charge or subject to a contribution towards the cost.

There is a list of allowable expenses (dependent upon the status of the defendant and his or her liabilities) which are deducted from the earned income and savings etc. If the resulting figure is above a certain sum, the defendant must contribute towards the cost of legal aid and a formula is employed to determine the amount of that contribution.

Contributions are divided into weekly sums which you must pay until your case is finally dealt with by a court. After that your contributions cease. If the eventual bill submitted to the Law Society by your solicitor or barrister is lower than the amount you have paid in contributions, the surplus will be returned to you by the court. Usually, however, your legal representative's bill will exceed your contributions by a considerable sum. You will not be required to pay the difference.

Key Terms

■ **Legal aid** Legal representation either free of charge or upon payment of a small contribution

Your solicitor may apply for legal aid whether you intend to plead not guilty or guilty. If legal aid is granted, your solicitor will either represent you at your trial or, if you plead guilty, will address the court on your behalf. If you plead not guilty and the case against you is dismissed, your solicitor may apply to the court to have some or all of any contributions you may have made refunded.

In practice, even though in terms of income/savings etc. you may qualify for legal aid, it is not often granted for motoring offences. You are, for example, very unlikely to be granted legal aid when charged with driving without due care and attention or for a straightforward case of driving with excess alcohol.

Legal aid may be granted if you are charged with a more serious offence such as dangerous driving and may be granted in cases involving excess alcohol when there is some risk of a custodial sentence – either because the reading is very high or because you have a previous conviction or convictions for a similar offence within the last ten years.

Not Guilty Pleas

The fact that legal aid is refused is not a good reason for pleading guilty if you believe you have a defence to the charge.

If you cannot afford to pay a solicitor to defend you, you should defend yourself. This is neither as difficult nor as traumatic as you may imagine, particularly since most courts operate a **duty solicitor** scheme. The duty solicitor will not defend you at your trial but will advise you how best to conduct your defence.

Key Terms

■ **Duty solicitor** A solicitor available to give advice without charge to defendants in court

Before looking at procedure, however, it is worth noting that a great many unrepresented defendants plead not guilty, believing that they have a defence to the charge when, in law, they do not. A common example is that of a defendant charged with an **excise licence** offence where the DVLA makes a claim for a considerable sum in back duty. Having pleaded not guilty, the defendant will readily admit to using a vehicle without a current tax disc. The correct course is to plead guilty to that charge and only then dispute the claim for back duty.

Similarly, unrepresented defendants will plead not guilty to exceeding the speed limit and then go on to admit that they were driving in excess of the 70 m.p.h. speed limit on a motorway, while denying that their speed was anything like the 95 m.p.h. alleged by the police. Again, the correct course is to plead guilty to the charge and only then to dispute the police evidence of the actual speed.

Apart from being a waste of everyone's time, not least your own, the effect of pleading not guilty and having an unnecessary trial is that when, inevitably, you are convicted, you will have to pay substantially greater prosecution costs. Courts, too, are required to take account of a prompt guilty plea when sentencing, giving a 'discount' of about a third on the sentence. If you plead not guilty without good reason, when, inevitably, you are convicted, you may find that the penalty is much greater than you had expected.

If you have not taken legal advice, be absolutely sure that you have a defence before you plead not guilty.

Key Terms

■ **Excise licence** A tax disc

If, having thought the matter through carefully, you propose to plead not guilty, there is no point in attending court on the date shown on the summons. Your case will not be heard on that date. You should complete and return to the court the 'notice of intention to plead not guilty' form and advise the court of any dates, say during the following eight weeks, when you and any witnesses you may wish to call will be unavailable. So that the court staff can estimate the length of time necessary for your hearing, you should advise the court of the number of witnesses you intend to call. You will be advised of the date set aside for the trial.

(The exception to the above is when you wish to plead not guilty to a charge of having no insurance, no driving licence or no MOT certificate. Simply send the document to the court with your not guilty plea or attend court on the date shown on the summons and produce the document. Provided that the prosecution finds it in order, the charge will be dismissed.)

In the intervening weeks, the prosecution may send you copies of one or more statements from witnesses. Quite often the evidence in these statements will not be in dispute. You will have seven days to decide whether or not that is the case. If you accept these statements they will simply be read out in court. The person providing the statement will not be required to attend.

If, however, you dispute any part of the evidence in the statements or believe that an explanation or clarification is necessary, you must advise the prosecution that you do not accept the statements and the witness(es) will attend court. If, for example, it is your defence that you were not present at the place on the date and time shown, you must not accept any statement that says you were.

In deciding whether or not to accept statements, however, there is a further implication to consider. If you choose to refuse statements and the person providing them duly appears in court, if you are subsequently found guilty you may find that you have to pay a greater sum in costs.

DUTY SOLICITOR SCHEME

Most courts operate a **duty solicitor** scheme. This represents an opportunity for you to take legal advice at no cost to yourself. The duty solicitor will advise you whether you have a defence to the charge. If it is believed that you have a defence, although the duty solicitor will not defend you at your trial you will be advised on how best to present your defence.

Often, you may be advised that what you believe is a defence is not a defence in law – and that you should plead guilty. Take this advice. If you do, the duty solicitor will address the court on your behalf, putting forward such extenuating circumstances as may persuade the magistrates to be as lenient as possible.

You are well advised to take advantage of this opportunity and, if you wish to do so, you should arrive at court early as other defendants will also wish to see the duty solicitor. The receptionist or an usher (an officer of the court readily identified because he or she is the only person in court who wears a gown) will advise you whether or not there is a duty solicitor available and will arrange for you to have an appointment.

Key Terms

■ **Duty solicitor** A solicitor available to give advice without charge to defendants in court

PROCEDURE BEFORE THE MAGISTRATES' COURT

If you are attending court in response to a summons, you will be required to attend at a stated time. It is possible, but unlikely, that your case will be heard immediately. You must, however, be there on time. If you are not, provided that the magistrates are satisifed that you are aware of the date and time of the proceedings, they may decide to commence hearing the case without you.

If you are **bailed** to attend at, say, 10.00 a.m. and arrive at 11.00 a.m. without a very good reason, you may be charged with an offence under the Bail Act and have to pay a fine. If you are bailed to attend and do not attend at all, the magistrates are likely to issue a warrant for your immediate arrest. When you do appear in court, unless you offer a really good explanation you are likely to be charged with failing to answer to your bail and will have to pay a fine or serve a short term of imprisonment.

Whether you are bailed or summoned to attend, if you cannot come or are going to be late you should telephone the court and explain the circumstances.

The usher will show you where you may sit and wait until your case is called. If you wish, you may sit in the courtroom and observe the earlier proceedings.

Present in court will be the following people.

Key Terms

■ **Bail** Release from custody with a duty to surrender to a court at a later date

The Magistrates

Usually three, though some larger courts have stipendiary magistrates, who are legally qualified, either barristers or solicitors, and who sit alone. The correct form of address is 'Your worships' and the chair or presiding magistrate is addressed as 'Sir' or 'Madam', not 'Your Honour' (a Crown Court judge) or 'Your Lordship' (a High Court judge).

The Court Clerk

An officer of the court, often a barrister or solicitor, whose function is to advise the magistrates on matters of law and to ensure that the proceedings are properly conducted and in the best interests of justice.

The Prosecutor

Your adversary, always a barrister or solicitor employed or instructed by the Crown Prosecution Service.

Members of the Public, Possibly the Press

A word about reporters. Occasionally a defendant will ask the court if the press may be instructed not to publish details of the case, fearing adverse publicity such as the headline in a local newspaper which read: 'Vicar convicted of Drink Driving'. You should know that the court has no power to make such an order.

When your case is called, the usher will show you where to stand and the clerk will read out the charge or charges.

Assuming that there is no **either way** matter, you will be asked whether you plead guilty or not guilty. When you have pleaded not guilty, the prosecutor will outline the facts to the court and may address the magistrates on the law relating to the offence or offences.

The prosecutor will then proceed to read out such statements as have been agreed by yourself and to call witnesses. Each witness will take the oath to tell the truth etc. and then give their evidence. When that evidence is concluded, you may wish to cross-examine, i.e. ask whatever questions you believe appropriate.

The rules of evidence are complex and you may have difficulty phrasing questions in a way which complies with those rules. In this respect you may expect assistance from the court clerk. Strictly impartial, the clerk will help you to frame questions and, if it appears that you have overlooked an important point, may ask a question on your behalf.

It is likely that one or more police officers will give evidence. A police officer will wish to refer to notes made at the time of the alleged offence and will ask the court for permission to do so. Provided such notes were written up as soon as practicable after the incident, you have no grounds for objecting, but you are entitled to ask to see those notes before the police officer refers to them.

When all the statements have been read and all the prosecution witnesses have given their evidence, the prosecution case is concluded. You will then have the opportunity to give evidence and to call witnesses to give evidence on your behalf. The prosecutor will cross-examine. When you conclude your case, you will have the chance to sum up the evidence for the benefit of the magistrates.

Key Terms

■ **Either way offence** An offence which may be tried either by a magistrates' court or before a judge and jury at a Crown Court

The magistrates will almost certainly retire to consider their verdict. Upon their return, the presiding magistrate will announce a finding of either not guilty or guilty. If found not guilty, you may make an application for **costs**. Include travelling expenses for yourself and your witnesses. If you or any of your witnesses have taken time off work to attend and have lost pay, you should claim that also.

If you are found guilty, the prosecutor will similarly apply for the prosecution's costs. Where the offence is **endorsable**, you will be required to surrender your driving licence to the court. Before you are sentenced you will have a further opportunity to address the court. Draw attention to any circumstances that are in your favour, circumstances that may persuade the magistrates to be lenient. If you are unemployed or in receipt of a low income, be sure that the court is aware of this.

Most motoring offenders are dealt with by way of a fine. If that is the sentence of the court, and you cannot afford to pay the fine and the prosecution costs at once, make the court an offer to pay so much per week, per fortnight or per month. Be sure that your offer is realistic. If it is not, the court will set a figure.

Finally, if the offence is endorsable and provided the magistrates do not disqualify you from driving, your licence will be endorsed by the court and returned to you by post. For disqualification and other possible penalties, see Chapter 11.

Key Terms

■ **Endorsement** The annotation of your driving licence with penalty points ■ **Costs** The cost of bringing a case to court

Guilty Pleas

GUILTY PLEAS IN ABSENCE

Thousands, perhaps tens of thousands, or motoring offenders a year attend court on the date specified on the summons
and plead guilty without realising that they may plead guilty
without attending court. Why? Because they read the summons and do not take the trouble to read the accompanying
documents. If the documents which accompany the summons include a written plea of guilty form, you may plead
guilty without attending court.

The form reads as on pages 174–5.

MAGISTRATES' COURTS ACT, 1980
NOTICE OF INTENTION TO ATTEND COURT (PART A)
or
NOTICE OF PLEA OF GUILTY (PART B)

From: A. N. OTHER
   15 STATION HILL   Case Number M00000
   MILTOWN
   STAFFORDSHIRE   Date 12/9/94

              Date of Hearing 11/10/94

Court MARKET CROSS, MILTOWN, STAFFS

Charge(s)

PLEASE COMPLETE **EITHER** PART A OR PART B

NOTES:
1. If you intend to consult a Solicitor you would be well advised to do so before completing this form.
2. Even if you complete Part A or Part B and return this form to the Clerk of the Court you may change your mind at any time before the hearing. If you do change your mind, notify the Clerk to the Court at once.
3. This form, when completed, should be returned as soon as possible to the Clerk of the Court at the address shown on the attached summons.

PART A. NOTICE OF INTENTION TO ATTEND COURT
1. Do you intend to deny the charge or one of the charges Yes/No
 (If so, please see the enclosed notice from the Clerk of the Court.) Please indicate which charges are denied ....
 I shall be calling .... Witnesses (Insert number of witnesses).
 Please list all inconvenient dates for you and your witnesses
 It is not convenient to attend court on the following dates:-

 Estimated length of case..
          Signed ....

---

2. I intend to admit the charge(s)   Signed ....

PART B. NOTICE OF WRITTEN PLEA OF GUILTY

I have read the Statement of Facts relating to the above charge(s).
I PLEAD GUILTY TO THE CHARGE(S) and I desire that the Court should dispose of the case in my absence.
I wish to bring to the Court's attention the mitigating circumstances set out overleaf.

       Signed ....
       Address..
           ....
           ....

A person giving notification in writing that he pleads guilty to an offence involving endorsement of driving licences or disqualification is required by Section 104(2) of the Road Traffic Act, 1972, to furnish information about his date of birth and sex.

Date of Birth		
Please Tick	Male	Female

Complete this part if there is a form accompanying these documents from the Vehicle Licensing Authority alleging 'Back Duty' is payable.

*a I do not wish to challenge the amount of back duty which is alleged to be due.
*b The amount specified in the notice is inappropriate for the following reason (Note, if you wish to prove that the amount is inappropriate it will normally be necessary for you to appear in Court with any witnesses or documents which may help to prove this).

*Delete (a) or (b)   Signed ....

Mitigating Circumstances

a) About the offence.

b) About my financial circumstances.

WEEKLY INCOME   WEEKLY EXPENSES

All you have to do is complete Part B and return it to the clerk to the justices at the address shown on the summons. If the offence, or one of the offences to which you plead guilty, is **endorsable** you must enclose your driving licence.

Note that you may change your guilty plea at any time before the hearing and may do so either by notifying the clerk or by attending court in person on the date shown on the summons and pleading not guilty. Your guilty plea will then be disregarded.

There is a space on the written plea of guilty form where you may write whatever you wish about the offence and about your financial circumstances. You should take advantage of this and may either write in the space provided or append a letter. A good letter may have the effect of considerably reducing a fine and, when the offence is endorsable and the number of penalty points is variable (e.g. exceeding the speed limit or driving without due care and attention), your letter may persuade the magistrates to impose fewer penalty points.

Court Procedure

When your case is called, the clerk will confirm that your guilty plea has been received. The clerk or the prosecutor will read out the **statement of facts**, a copy of which was among the documents you received with the summons, and, before the court decides on an appropriate sentence, the clerk will read out what you have written.

Key Terms

■ **Endorsement** The annotation of your driving licence with penalty points ■ **Statement of facts** A document accompanying a summons

Before we look at letters, however, we will look at some circumstances in which the court will be unable to deal with your case.

1. If you write anything which could amount to a defence to the charge

A DEFENDANT was charged with failing to produce her driving licence and wrote, 'I plead guilty to the charge. I was married recently and sent my licence to the DVLA to have the name changed. It was not returned in time for me to produce it at the police station within the seven days allowed. Though I produced it later, I was told that I was too late.'

The court will not accept this guilty plea because what the defendant has written amounts to a defence to the charge.

2. If you disagree substantially with the statement of facts.

If you plead guilty without attending court, you accept that the statement of facts is broadly correct.

A DEFENDANT was charged with exceeding the speed limit and wrote, 'I accept that I was exceeding the 70 m.p.h. speed limit on the motorway but my speed was nothing like the 97 m.p.h. alleged in the statement of facts – more like 87 m.p.h.'

The court is likely to order this defendant to attend so that evidence may be heard from prosecution witnesses, and

Key Terms

■ **Statement of facts** A document accompanying a summons

from the defendant and any witnesses the defendant may wish to call in order to determine which version of events is correct. If you do not attend, the court will accept the prosecution version.

3. If the court is considering disqualification

If, despite what you write, the court is considering disqualification, your case will be adjourned and you will receive a notice requiring your attendance and advising you of the reason. Note that the court which receives your written plea of guilty will not disqualify you in your absence. So, even though you believe that disqualification is inevitable, plead guilty in absence and write a letter to the court. You have nothing to lose. You must, however, attend court if you receive a notice of adjournment for consideration of disqualification. If you do not attend, provided the court is satisfied that you received the notice in time it will either issue a warrant for your arrest or impose a disqualification in your absence.

LETTERS TO THE COURT

Be clear about the purpose of your letter. It is to persuade the court to impose a lesser penalty. The first rule is: be sure that what you write is legible. Surprisingly often the odd word here and there cannot be deciphered. Occasionally the entire letter is illegible. If you cannot write legibly, type the letter or get someone to type it for you.

The second rule is: keep your letter brief and to the point. Letters running into three or four pages are not uncommon. Such letters impress neither the unfortunate clerk who has to read them nor the magistrates who are obliged to listen. Here is a typical example. The defendant pleads guilty to a charge of driving without due care and attention.

Dear Sirs,

I acknowledge receipt of the summons and wish to plead guilty to the allegation of driving without due care and attention. The circumstances of the offence were as follows.

At 4.30 p.m. on the afternoon of Wednesday, January 14th, I was driving west along Park Lane and wished to turn right into Market Street. As I approached the junction I could see that the traffic lights were red so I stopped and moved forward when the lights changed to green. There were vehicles, including large lorries, coming in all directions. I particularly recollect a large furniture van that obscured my view.

Anyway, I waited for some time until I thought I saw a gap in the oncoming traffic and then I commenced my right turn – only to be hit by another vehicle on the rear nearside. I accept that I was responsible for the collision (and am therefore pleading guilty) but to this day I honestly do not know where the other vehicle came from. I thought I had taken all the steps necessary to accomplish my manoeuvre safely. Wherever it came from it must have been going too fast for the prevailing road conditions.

Fortunately, damage was not extensive and, of course, you will know that no one was injured. The police arrived on the scene and one of the officers told me that this particular junction is a well known 'accident black-spot'. I understand that there have been accidents which have resulted in serious injury and damage much more extensive than that sustained in this incident.

I apologise to the court for the incident and confess that on this occasion the standard of my driving fell far below its usual standard. May I add that I have not been involved in an accident of any sort for more than 15 years – and, even then, the accident was not my fault.

As my car is insured third party only, I have had to pay a considerable sum to have it repaired. I trust that in those circumstances the court will fine me as little as possible and allow me to pay that fine at the rate of £5 per week.

I understand that my licence will have to be endorsed with penalty points and that these may be anything from 3 to 9. I urge the court to consider what I have said above and to be as lenient as possible.

Yours faithfully

This is a poor letter, mainly because it is much too long. The magistrates are likely to lose interest after the first couple of paragraphs. If it is to be effective, you must make it very much shorter.

Delete the first paragraph. It is perfectly clear that you have received the summons and, since you have completed the notice of written plea of guilty form, it is clear that you are pleading guilty. Neither is there any need to go into detail about the incident. The court have heard the statement of facts. The magistrates know when, where and how the accident occurred.

Instead, tell the magistrates something they do not know. Draw their attention to circumstances which may not be obvious from the statement of facts.

For example, it was dusk, so 'visibility was poor'. Traffic was coming in all directions: 'Traffic was heavy.' Why did you have an accident? Because you made 'an error of judgement'. What was the extent of the damage? Was anyone injured? 'Damage was slight and no one was injured.'

Think about the last three paragraphs of the letter. Is the court really likely to be interested in what happened 15 years ago? Do the magistrates really wish to know about your problem with third party insurance? You offer to pay the fine at the rate of £5 a week. Support this request with details of your income and expenditure.

This defendant would be well advised to write to the court along these lines instead:

Dear Sirs

I wish to draw the attention of the court to the following exten-
uating circumstances. Visibility was poor, traffic was heavy.
Damage was slight and no one was injured.

I have held a clean driving licence for 15 years, regret that this
incident occurred and ask the court to be as lenient as possible.

I append details of my income and expenditure. Please may I
pay the fine at the rate of £5 per week?

Yours faithfully

Unhelpful Comments

It is surprising how often defendants write something
unhelpful, something that may have the effect of increasing
the penalty rather than decreasing it. A phrase which is commonly used is 'I was not familiar with the vehicle'.

A defendant was charged with exceeding the speed limit
and wrote: 'My own car was in for servicing and the garage
loaned me a car which was much more powerful. Obviously,
I was not familiar with the vehicle and had no idea I was
driving quite so fast.'

A large number of people regard this as an extenuating
circumstance. Even solicitors use the excuse from time to
time. The court, however, is likely to take a different view. It
really amounts to the fact that you were driving a vehicle
with which you were not familiar at an excessive speed. Does
it sound quite so good now?

Another not uncommon one is: 'Sorry, I was chatting
and didn't notice my speed creeping up.' It would be better
to write nothing at all.

`I drive for a living' or 'I am a professional driver' are
commonly used phrases but you should think very carefully
before using one of them. When the number of penalty
points to be imposed is variable, at the discretion of the

magistrates, you may write something like: 'I drive for a living and therefore ask the court to endorse my driving licence with the minimum number of points.' The court may, however, take the view that a somewhat higher standard of driving is to be expected from a professional driver. . .

You will not, of course, be so stupid as to write something like: 'I think it is a pity that the police have nothing better to do.'

Never mention the word 'disqualification'. It is pointless. The court will not disqualify you in your absence. See **adjournment notices** for consideration of disqualification (on page 182). The magistrates may not even be considering such a penalty. Why draw their attention to it?

The number of penalty points which a court may impose for two of the more common offences, exceeding the speed limit and careless driving, is variable. Do not suggest that in your case the appropriate number of penalty points should be 3 or 4 or whatever number comes to mind. What do you know about it?

Rely on the extenuating circumstances you describe in your letter to influence the court's decision. You may write: 'In view of the extenuating circumstances I have put forward, I ask the court to impose as few penalty points as possible.'

Finally, if you cannot afford to pay the likely fine at once, do not simply ask for time to pay. Do that, and the court may well give you 28 days in which to pay the full amount. Make the court an offer of so much per week, per fortnight or per month. Support your request with details of your income and expenditure. The court will often accept a realistic offer.

Key Terms

■ **Adjournment notice** A notice advising that the case has been adjourned to a particular date

Having taken a look at the sort of thing you should not write, what circumstances may persuade the court to impose a smaller fine or, where possible, to order fewer penalty points?

IN GENERAL

If you have never before been convicted of a motoring offence, say so. If you have held a clean driving licence for a number of years, say so.

Most commonly, defendants write to the court when pleading guilty to one of the following charges:

- exceeding the speed limit;
- driving without due care and attention;
- vehicle defect offences;
- failing to produce documents.

Exceeding the Speed Limit

Often you will have been offered the option of paying a **fixed penalty** but for some reason, often because your driving licence was at the DVLA, you were unable to take advantage of that option. Be sure the court is aware that you were offered that option and of the reason why you were unable to

Key Terms

■ **Fixed penalty** Provides an opportunity to have the matter dealt with other than by a court

take advantage of it. The magistrates may be lenient, impose a fine equivalent to the fixed penalty and order no more than the minimum number of penalty points.

Why were you speeding? If you had a good reason, give that reason. For example, a passenger in your vehicle may have been feeling unwell, you may have been hurrying home because your wife was ill or to see a sick child. If you are able to support what you write with documentary evidence – a medical certificate or a letter from a doctor – so much the better.

You may have been driving to an important business meeting and been unexpectedly delayed, perhaps by road-works or a breakdown. A letter from your employer or from a business associate confirming the importance of the meeting would be helpful.

If the weather was fine and visibility good, say so. If traffic was light, say so. A court will usually take a less serious view of a speeding offence committed on a deserted road in the early hours of the morning.

Driving Without Due Care and Attention

You should consider carefully whether it is in your interest to draw the attention of the court to weather and/or traffic conditions. For example, if you drove into the rear of another vehicle in the centre of town and the weather was awful, the visibility poor, the road slippery, say so. If, in those circumstances, traffic was heavy, say so.

On the other hand, there are circumstances in which it is to your advantage to point out that traffic was light.

If the charge was brought because you were involved in an accident, if damage was minimal and no one was injured, say so. If, immediately before the accident, the sun was in your eyes or you were dazzled by the headlights of an oncoming vehicle, say so. If your view was obscured by a hedgerow, a pedestrian or another vehicle, say so.

Consider carefully what is in your favour and what is not. Above all, if there can be any doubt about it, make it clear to the court that the offence was caused by an error of judgement or a momentary lapse of concentration and not by deliberate bad driving.

Vehicle Defects

You may have been issued with a **VDRS** notice. If you failed to take advantage of that opportunity and received a **summons**, perhaps you had a good excuse. Perhaps your vehicle required a part which was ordered but which did not arrive in time. Possibly you were issued with a **fixed penalty** notice but were unable to take advantage of that opportunity because the offence is **endorsable** and you were unable to produce your driving licence within seven days.

If you were offered either of these options and failed to take advantage of them, explain the circumstances in your letter to the court.

The person responsible for the defect is the person using the vehicle at the time of the offence. If it was not your vehicle, say so. This does not represent a defence to the charge but it may help to limit the penalty.

Failing to Produce Documents

An extraordinary number of motorists fail to produce documents within the time allowed and have to pay a fine for

---

Key Terms

■ **VDRS** A scheme whereby a motorist is given an opportunity to put right vehicle defects without penalty ■ **Summons** The document which begins most court proceedings ■ **Fixed penalty** Provides an opportunity to have the matter dealt with other than by a court ■ **Endorsement** The annotation of your driving licence with penalty points

each document not produced. If you take the advice offered in Chapter 1 and keep your driving documents with you at all times, you cannot commit this offence.

It is a defence to the charge that it was not reasonably practicable to produce a document within the time allowed, provided that you produced it as soon as possible. You may have sent your driving licence to the DVLA for change of address. If you drive a company car, you may not be able to obtain an insurance certificate within the time allowed.

If none of the above apply and you plead guilty, write to the court and explain why you failed to produce the document. Perhaps you were called away unexpectedly. You may have asked someone else to produce the document for you – and they forgot. You may have produced a photocopy or a fax and the police would not accept it.

If you fail to produce a document, the prosecution will assume that you do not have one. There will be two charges. For example you may receive a **summons** alleging that you failed to produce your insurance certificate and that you used a vehicle without insurance. These are alternative charges – if you do not have an insurance certificate, you can hardly be expected to produce it.

Assuming that you were insured, you must send the insurance certificate to the court with a not guilty plea. If you do not, the court will convict you of the more serious charge and, almost certainly, order you to attend because the magistrates have disqualification from driving in mind.

Key Terms

■ **Summons** The document which begins most court proceedings

GUILTY PLEAS IN PERSON

If you intend to plead guilty, assuming that the documents which accompanied the summons included a **guilty plea in absence form**, why do you wish to attend? Generally it is pointless and time-consuming. You will be required to attend at a particular time. If you are very fortunate, your case will be heard immediately. It is much more likely, however, that you will have to wait, possibly for some hours. Yet you must be there on time. If you are not, the court may deal with your case without you.

Remember, too, that if you are present in court, the prosecutor is no longer restricted to the **statement of facts**. He may go into greater detail. If this could prove embarrassing, plead guilty by letter.

There are, however, two circumstances in which, though you intend to plead guilty, you must attend court:

1. when you disagree substantially with the statement of facts;

2. when you wish to put forward **special reasons** for not endorsing your driving licence.

Disagreeing with the Statement of Facts

If you plead guilty by letter, the court will rely on the statement of facts when deciding on an appropriate penalty. Even

---

Key Terms

■ **Guilty in absence** A guilty plea by post or otherwise in the absence of the defendant ■ **Statement of facts** A document accompanying a summons ■ **Special reasons** Reasons special to the circumstances of the offence which allow a court a discretion not to endorse or not to disqualify

though you are clearly guilty of the offence, you may wish to challenge those facts. You may only do so by attending court. You should advise the clerk to the justices of your intention so that a date may be set aside for a hearing. In order that the court staff may have some idea of the length of time to allow, advise the court of how many witnesses you intend to call. The matter will be adjourned to a convenient date.

The court will hear evidence from the prosecution, and from yourself and your witnesses, in order to determine the correct version of events. If the court is satisfied that your version is correct, the sentence imposed will be one appropriate to that version.

A MOTORIST was charged with crossing a double white line and the statement of facts alleged that he drove on the wrong side of the double white line for a distance of 50 m. A police officer gave evidence confirming that he had observed the vehicle and had estimated the distance travelled in contravention of the system at 50 m.

The motorist gave evidence that immediately before the double white line system he had overtaken a slow-moving vehicle and was unable to regain the correct side of the road before crossing the double white line. He did so as quickly as possible and maintained that the distance he travelled in contravention of the double white line system was no more than 20 m. Called as a witness, a passenger in the vehicle gave similar evidence.

The court preferred the evidence given by the defence.

A DEFENDANT was charged with exceeding the speed limit. The statement of facts alleged a speed of 51 m.p.h. over a distance of 500 m on a road where speed is restricted to 30 m.p.h. The defendant pleaded guilty but disputed the speed. The driver of a police Panda car gave evidence that he had observed the defendant's vehicle drive by and had formed the opinion that the speed was in excess of the limit. He had followed the vehicle over the distance stated and recorded a speed between 48 and 51 m.p.h. He caused the vehicle to stop.

The driver and his passenger said in evidence that they had seen the police car parked beside the road and the driver had immediately braked, reducing his speed from about 40 m.p.h. to 30 m.p.h.

The court preferred the evidence given by the defence.

Special reasons for not endorsing

If you plead guilty to an offence for which penalty points must be imposed, there are limited circumstances in which you may be able to argue **special reasons** for not imposing those points.

The fact that an offence is trivial is not a special reason. The fact that endorsement would result in disqualification under the **totting-up** provisions and that the defendant requires a licence for the purpose of carrying on his or her business is not a special reason. The fact that a motorist was not aware that he or she was breaking the law is not a special reason.

A special reason is one that is special to the circumstances in which the offence was committed, not to the circumstances of the defendant. It must fulfil four requirements:

Key Terms

■ **Special reasons** Reasons special to the circumstances of the offence which allow a court a discretion not to endorse or not to disqualify ■ **Totting up** The adding together of the number of valid penalty points on your driving licence

1. it must be an extenuating circumstance;

2. it must not amount to a defence to the charge;

3. it must be directly connected with the commission of the offence;

4. it must be a matter which the court may properly take into account when sentencing.

Special reasons are most often found:

1. when the offence is committed while the defendant is coping with a real emergency;

2. when the offence is committed while the defendant is driving a short distance;

3. when the defendant has been misled in some way.

A motorist who was concerned about his passenger's health exceeded the speed limit. His solicitor successfully argued special reasons.

A disqualified driver who drove his car a few yards from the road into the driveway of his house successfully argued special reasons.

A motorist who realised that he was under the influence of drink decided not to drive his car and telephoned for a taxi. Waiting for the taxi, he fell asleep in his car. When the motorist was subsequently charged with 'Being in charge of a vehicle with excess alcohol', his solicitor successfully argued special reasons.

A FATHER arranged for his son to drive his car by including his name on his (the father's) insurance policy. This, however, increased the premium very substantially and, when the father was made redundant, he told his son that when the policy was due for renewal on 30 March, he would be obliged to have his son's name removed and his son would have to make his own arrangements.

The son was stopped while driving on 25 March and discovered that the renewal date was not 30 March but 20 March. He was charged with using a vehicle without insurance, attended court with his father and saw the **duty solicitor**. The duty solicitor advised him to plead guilty but pleaded special reasons for not endorsing his licence. The son and the father gave evidence on oath and the court took the view that an honest mistake had been made. He had to pay a fine plus prosecution costs but his driving licence was not endorsed.

Further examples of special reasons are given under the relevant offences.

In addition to special reasons for not **endorsing**, a court may find special reasons for not disqualifying even though disqualification is obligatory. Most commonly, special reasons for not disqualifying are found in cases involving excess alcohol (see Chapter 7).

If you believe that you may have special reasons, you should consult a solicitor or ask to see the duty solicitor.

When You Are Ordered to Attend

The above are the circumstances in which you may choose to attend court, even though you intend to plead guilty. There are also circumstances in which you have no choice – you are ordered to attend. You may have been charged with one of the more serious offences (e.g. driving with excess alcohol) and **bailed** to attend, or you may have been

---

Key Terms

■ **Duty solicitor** A solicitor available to give advice without charge to defendants in court ■ **Endorsement** The annotation of your driving licence with penalty points ■ **Bail** Release from custody with a duty to surrender to a court at a later date

ordered to attend because the court which received your written plea of guilty adjourned your case for consideration of disqualification.

Attendance for consideration of disqualification

You will have been ordered to attend either because the court has disqualification in mind for the offence or because the penalty points applicable to this latest offence make you liable for disqualification under the **totting up** provisions.

You must attend court in response to such a notice. If you do not, provided the court is satisfied that you have received the notice in time, either a warrant will be issued for your arrest or you may be disqualified in your absence. Your chances of avoiding disqualification will not be good and you would be very unwise to drive yourself to court alone. A great many over-optimistic defendants have found themselves and their vehicles stranded in such circumstances...

If you are disqualified, the period of disqualification begins immediately.

Key Terms

■ **Totting up** The adding together of the number of valid penalty points on your driving licence

****** MAGISTRATES' COURT

NOTICE OF ADJOURNMENT   CASE No (   )

(DISCRETIONARY DISQUALIFICATION)

THE CASE HAS BEEN ADJOURNED AFTER
CONVICTION TO GIVE YOU AN OPPORTUNITY
TO APPEAR IN PERSON TO PUT FORWARD
REPRESENTATIONS AS TO WHY YOU SHOULD NOT
BE DISQUALIFIED FOR THE OFFENCE.

FAILURE TO APPEAR MAY RESULT IN A
DISQUALIFICATION BEING IMPOSED IN YOUR
ABSENCE OR A WARRANT BEING ISSUED FOR YOUR
ARREST.

YOUR CASE WILL BE HEARD ON (DATE) AT (TIME).

YOU ARE REQUESTED TO SIGN AND RETURN THE
ACKNOWLEDGEMENT BELOW. ANY
CORRESPONDENCE REGARDING THIS MATTER
SHOULD BE ADDRESSED TO THE CLERK TO THE
JUSTICES AND SHOULD QUOTE THE CASE NUMBER.

I acknowledge receipt of the Notice of Adjournment informing me
of the hearing at the above named court at (time) on (date).

Signed

Date

****** MAGISTRATES' COURT

NOTICE OF ADJOURNMENT   CASE No ( )

(THE TOTTING UP PROVISIONS)

IT HAS BEEN NOTED FROM ENDORSEMENTS
RECORDED AGAINST YOU THAT YOU ARE LIABLE TO
BE DISQUALIFIED FROM DRIVING BY VIRTUE OF
SECTION 35 OF THE ROAD TRAFFIC OFFENDERS ACT
1988.

THE CASE HAS BEEN ADJOURNED AFTER
CONVICTION TO GIVE YOU AN OPPORTUNITY TO
APPEAR IN PERSON TO PUT FORWARD
REPRESENTATIONS AS TO WHY YOU SHOULD NOT BE
DISQUALIFIED.

FAILURE TO APPEAR MAY RESULT IN A
DISQUALIFICATION BEING IMPOSED IN YOUR
ABSENCE OR A WARRANT BEING ISSUED FOR YOUR
ARREST.

YOUR CASE WILL BE HEARD ON (DATE) AT (TIME).

YOU ARE REQUESTED TO SIGN AND RETURN THE
ACKNOWLEDGEMENT BELOW. ANY
CORRESPONDENCE REGARDING THIS MATTER
SHOULD BE ADDRESSED TO THE CLERK TO THE
JUSTICES AND SHOULD QUOTE THE CASE NUMBER.

I acknowledge receipt of the Notice of Adjournment informing me
of the hearing at the above named court at (time) on (date).

Signed

Date

DISQUALIFICATION FOR THE OFFENCE

Upon conviction for some of the more serious offences, disqualification is obligatory. The magistrates have no choice. Where, however, you have pleaded **guilty in absence** to an offence and have subsequently been ordered to attend, disqualification is at the discretion of the court. The magistrates do have a choice. If you are to persuade them not to disqualify, you must put forward all the extenuating circumstances described under guilty pleas in absence.

If disqualification will have a serious effect on your ability to work, you should make sure that the court is aware of that. Support your claim with a letter from your employer.

You should consider whether or not you should be represented by a solicitor.

Exceeding the Speed Limit

If you drive at 100 m.p.h. or more on a motorway you are at high risk of disqualification.

This principle also applies to other roads. If you drive at a speed of 30 m.p.h. above the legal limit, you are likely to be disqualified. You should know, however, that motorists have been disqualified for driving at lesser speeds. The court will take into account such factors as weather conditions, visibility and traffic conditions. In some circumstances you may drive at 55 m.p.h. in a built-up area and receive no

---

Key Terms

■ **Guilty in absence** A guilty plea by post or otherwise in the absence of the defendant

more than a **fixed penalty**. In other circumstances you may receive a **summons** and, upon conviction, be disqualified from driving.

The period of disqualification will depend upon the particular circumstances of your case, e.g. the time of day, whether traffic was heavy or light, whether visibility was good or poor etc. A disqualification for speeding is, however, likely to be for a short period:

30–35 m.p.h. above the legal limit	*7 days*
36–40 m.p.h. above the legal limit	*14 days*
45 m.p.h. above the legal limit	*21 days*

At speeds greater than the above, the period of disqualification will increase sharply. The period of disqualification may also be increased if you have a previous conviction for speeding.

Using a Vehicle Without Insurance

Courts take a serious view of driving without insurance. Unless you convince the court that the offence was not committed deliberately, i.e. that you did not drive knowing that you were uninsured, you are at high risk of disqualification for a period of some months. The period of disqualification will depend on the length of time you have been driving while uninsured and whether or not you have previous convictions for the same offence.

Drivers of HGV vehicles, taxis, minicabs etc. are likely to be treated more severely.

Key Terms

■ **Fixed penalty** Provides an opportunity to have the matter dealt with other than by a court ■ **Summons** The document which begins most court proceedings

Driving Without Due Care and Attention etc.

In theory at least, you may be disqualified for any **endorsable** offence. In practice, however, if you plead guilty in absence to a charge of careless driving, crossing a double white line, failing to observe a traffic signal etc., the magistrates would have to regard it as a particularly serious case to consider disqualification.

In considering what is serious and what is not, the court will have regard to the cause rather than the effect.

⚠ A MOTORIST who overtook a police car at 50 m.p.h. on a dual carriageway in fog and with visibility restricted to no more than 25 m was charged with driving without due care and attention. He pleaded guilty by letter but the court adjourned his case and ordered him to attend. He was fined £200, had to pay prosecution costs and was disqualified from driving for three months.

A motorist who stopped at a junction with a major road, intending to drive straight across when it was safe to do so, misjudged the speed of an oncoming vehicle. A collision occurred and, as a result, his rear seat passenger sustained fatal injuries. He attended court and pleaded guilty to driving without due care and attention. He was fined £200, had to pay prosecution costs and his licence was endorsed with 6 penalty points. He was not disqualified.

The principle of cause and effect is not well understood and apparent anomalies such as the above receive much adverse publicity in the press. For a more detailed explanation, see 'Driving without due care' on page 74.

Key Terms

■ **Endorsement** The annotation of your driving licence with penalty points

Disqualification under the Totting-up Procedure

You receive a summons and plead guilty by letter to an offence of, say, exceeding the speed limit, only to receive a notice from the court requiring you to attend for consideration of disqualification under the **totting-up** provisions.

Totting up means adding the number of penalty points which may be imposed for this most recent offence to the number of valid points already on your licence. Valid penalty points are those imposed for an offence committed in the three years immediately preceding the date when you committed the latest offence. If that total comes to 12 or more, you are liable for disqualification under the totting-up provisions.

A MOTORIST received a summons alleging that he exceeded the speed limit on 3 March 1991. He pleaded guilty by letter and, on 16 June 1991, his licence was endorsed with 3 penalty points. He received another summons alleging that he exceeded the speed limit on 8 October 1993. Again he pleaded guilty by letter and, on 26 December of that year, his licence was endorsed with a further 6 penalty points.

On 20 January 1994, he was stopped and a summons was issued alleging that he crossed a double white line. He pleaded guilty by letter on 14 April. Some days later, however, he received an **adjournment notice** in the post requiring him to attend court for consideration of disqualification from driving under the totting-up provisions.

Key Terms

■ **Totting up** The adding together of the number of valid penalty points on your driving licence ■ **Adjournment notice** A notice advising that the case has been adjourned to a particular date

The relevant dates are the dates on which the first and last offences were committed. The dates of the court appearances are irrelevant. A defendant who seeks adjournment after adjournment so that he or she finally appears in court more than three years after the date of the first relevant offence is wasting time . . .

In the example above, the last offence was committed within three years of the first one, so the defendant is liable for disqualification under the totting-up provisions.

It used to be the case that a disqualification even for a short period had the effect of removing all existing penalty points from the licence. When you had served your period of disqualification, you had a clean licence. The 1991 Road Traffic Act changed that. Now only a period of disqualification under the totting-up provisions has that effect.

If, however, you are disqualified for an offence, the penalty points ordered by the court which disqualifies you are purely nominal and do not count for totting-up purposes.

In the example above, if, in addition to the 6 penalty points ordered for the offence committed on 8 October, the defendant was disqualified from driving for a period of 14 days, those 6 penalty points would not count for totting-up purposes. When he pleaded guilty to the offence committed on 20 January, effectively the number of penalty points on his licence was 3 – those imposed for the offence committed on 3 March 1991. Totting up does not apply.

The minimum period of disqualification under the totting-up provisions is six months (there are circumstances in which the minimum period is 12 months or two years, see page 214).

If you receive a **notice of adjournment** requiring you to attend court for consideration of disqualification under the

---

Key Terms

■ **Adjournment notice** A notice advising that the case has been adjourned to a particular date

totting-up provisions, you must attend. If you do not, a warrant may be issued for your arrest or you may be disqualified in your absence.

Disqualification from driving under the totting-up provisions is not obligatory. The court has a limited discretion either not to disqualify you or to disqualify you for a period shorter than six months.

You will have to persuade the court that disqualification from driving would cause exceptional hardship.

Exceptional Hardship

If, as a result of being disqualified from driving for six months, you will lose your job, that is hardship. But hundreds of decided cases over the years have established the principle that such hardship is not in itself exceptional.

In order to prove exceptional hardship, you must demonstrate that disqualification would cause not only hardship to yourself, but hardship to an innocent third party. The third party may be, for example, a spouse or elderly relative, an employer or employee.

If you intend to plead exceptional hardship, either consult a solicitor or see the **duty solicitor**.

A YOUNG MAN worked as a tyre fitter and claimed that he was required to drive in connection with his work and that, if he was disqualified, he might well be dismissed.

The court did not find exceptional hardship.

Key Terms

■ **Duty solicitor** A solicitor available to give advice without charge to defendants in court

⚠ A SALES representative was married with a young son. His wife did not work and he had recently been appointed to his present position after a long period of unemployment. He was paying off arrears of his mortgage and a loan from his bank.

The court found exceptional hardship.

⚠ AN HGV DRIVER submitted to the court a letter from his employer to the effect that he had worked for the company for a number of years, and was a valued and trustworthy employee. The letter went on to say, however, that no work other than driving was available and that, if he were disqualified, the company would be obliged to dismiss him. The defendant gave evidence that he had been driving goods vehicles for 25 years and knew no other trade.

The court found exceptional hardship.

If the court does find exceptional hardship, the chairperson will announce the reason for that finding. You should know that if, within three years, you appear again before a court which has in mind disqualification under the totting-up provisions, you will not be permitted to use the same reasons.

Sentences and Orders

If you are convicted of a motoring offence, i.e. if you plead guilty or, after a trial, are found guilty, you will be required to pay a contribution towards the **costs** of the prosecution. In addition, the court will impose one or more of the following penalties according to the seriousness of the offence:

● an absolute or conditional discharge;

● a fine;

● a compensation order;

● a community penalty;

● a custodial sentence (i.e. a term of imprisonment).

And, when the offence is **endorsable**, one or more of the following:

● the endorsement of your driving licence with penalty points;

● disqualification from driving;

● an order to take a re-test;

● an order of forfeiture of your vehicle.

Key Terms

■ **Costs** The cost of bringing a case to court ■ **Endorsement** The annotation of your driving licence with penalty points

DISCHARGE

An absolute discharge means that, although a conviction is recorded, there is no penalty. A conditional discharge is granted for a period, say 12 months, and means that provided you commit no further offences within that period, there will be no penalty. If, however, you do commit an offence, in addition to sentencing you for that offence, the court may substitute some other penalty for the conditional discharge.

FINES

The vast majority of motoring offenders are dealt with by way of a fine. When deciding on the amount of the fine, the court will consider the seriousness of the offence and the means of the offender, i.e. ability to pay, income and expenditure, and any savings.

The Seriousness of the Offence

Magistrates are provided with guidelines suggesting the appropriate fine for a typical example of the offence. The fine will be increased if the court believes that the circumstances of the offence are more serious and decreased if the court believe that the circumstances are less serious.

Whether you have pleaded guilty in absence or are attending court, you should attempt to persuade the court to take as lenient a view as possible. Put forward whatever extenuating circumstances you can. Examples of what you should and should not say are given in Chapter 10.

The Means of the Offender

Since the Unit Fine system was abolished in October 1993, courts are no longer required to provide you with a Statement of Means Form. Most courts still do, some do not. If you have no savings and are unemployed or in receipt of a low income, it is absolutely essential that the court is made aware of your financial situation. Otherwise you may be fined very much more than you can afford to pay.

Complete a Statement of Means Form. If such a form is not provided, make a note of your income and expenditure on a piece of paper. If you are not in a position to pay the fine at once, the court will usually give you time to pay, if you ask. Whether sending a **guilty plea in absence** or attending court, it is not enough simply to ask for time to pay. Make it clear how much you believe you can afford to pay per week, per fortnight or per month: 'Please may I pay the fine at the rate of £x per fortnight?'

The court will generally accept a realistic offer. If your offer is not realistic, the magistrates will order you to pay at whatever rate they believe is realistic. Given time to pay, there is the facility to have your fine transferred to the magistrates' court nearest to your home address for convenience: 'Please may I have the fine transferred to X Magistrates' Court?'

What Will Happen If You Don't Pay

You may be summoned to appear before a fine default court or a distress warrant may be issued to seize your goods. If the distress warrant fails because you have insufficient

---

Key Terms

■ **Guilty in absence** A guilty plea by post or otherwise in the absence of the defendant

goods, a warrant for your arrest will be issued. The warrant may be with or without **bail**. If the former, you will be arrested and released with a duty to surrender to the court at a later date. If the latter, you will be arrested and will remain in police custody until you are brought before a court.

At court, you will be required to give evidence on oath about your means and are well advised to provide documentary evidence wherever possible. If it is clear that your means have deteriorated since the fine was imposed – if, for example, you have lost your job, the court has the power to remit, i.e. cancel – some or all of the outstanding amount, or to order you to pay at a reduced rate.

If your circumstances have changed for the worse, don't bury your head in the sand. Write to the court and explain why you can't pay.

If, on the other hand, the court takes the view that you have deliberately made no effort to pay the fine, the ultimate sanction is that you will be sentenced to a term of imprisonment. When you are released, the fine is considered paid.

COMPENSATION

A magistrates' court has the power to order compensation up to a maximum of £5000 per offence for injury or damage sustained during the commission of an offence. The most

---

Key Terms

■ **Bail** Release from custody with a duty to surrender to a court at a later date

common example in motoring matters is where damage is caused to a vehicle and the injured party has an excess on his or her insurance policy. A court may order a motorist convicted of, say, driving without due care and attention, to pay compensation in the sum of that excess.

The magistrates must be satisfied that compensation is justified and that the offender has the means to pay. Again, if you ask for time to pay, the court will usually agree and, in those circumstances, payments may be transferred to your nearest magistrates' court. You should be aware that, if you get into difficulties, the court has only limited powers to cancel a compensation order. If you are sentenced to a term of imprisonment for non-payment, the compensation will still be payable when you are released.

COMMUNITY PENALTIES

When a discharge or fine, often combined with one of the specific motoring penalties described below, e.g. endorsement of your driving licence or disqualification from driving, is not considered a sufficient penalty, a range of community sentences is available, usually upon conviction for offences punishable by a term of imprisonment.

Before sentencing, the court will require the Probation Service to prepare a pre-sentence report and an adjournment for up to four weeks will be necessary. The purpose of the report is to provide the magistrates with information about your character and background, and to make proposals as to the most appropriate sentence.

Preparation of the report will involve one or more interviews with a probation officer. It is very much in your interest to co-operate fully. If you have been convicted of an imprisonable offence and do not co-operate, for example if you persistently fail to keep appointments without very good reason, when you return to court you are at high risk of being sentenced to a term of imprisonment.

The community penalties most frequently imposed in motoring matters are:

1. a probation order;

2. a community service order;

3. a combination order.

A Probation Order

A probation order is made for a specific length of time, between six months and three years, during which you will be under the supervision of a probation officer. You must attend at the probation officer's office as and when you are instructed and must permit him or her to visit you at your home. You must advise your probation officer at once of any change of address or change of employment.

The order is often made with a condition that you attend a prescribed course. For example, upon conviction for an alcohol-related offence, the order may be made with a condition that you attend a particular adult alcohol education course or impaired drivers' course.

A Community Service Order

You will be required to perform unpaid work in the community for a specified number of hours up to a maximum of 240. You will be under the supervision of a community service officer, must be of good behaviour and must advise the officer of any change of address or change of employment. You must report for such work as and when you are instructed.

Suitable work may be anything from gardening or paint-
ing and decorating, to working with the elderly or with the
handicapped. If you are in employment, your supervising
officer will arrange suitable work in the evenings and/or at
weekends.

If you have practical skills, for example if you are a car-
penter or bricklayer, the court will regard such skills as being
of great benefit to the community. In those circumstances, if
you are convicted of an offence which is so serious that the
court is considering a term of imprisonment, you or your
solicitor may persuade the court to impose a community service order instead.

A Combination Order

This is one of the new sentences introduced by the Criminal
Justice Act 1991. It combines elements of a community service order with those of a probation order. You may, for
example, be placed on probation for 12 months and
required to do 80 hours' community service. You may be
sure that if the court has a combination order in mind, the
magistrates have taken a very serious view. You very nearly
went to prison . . .

Sentencing

When the reports have been prepared and you return to
court for sentence, the presiding magistrate will tell you
which community sentence the court has in mind, and will
explain the terms and conditions of the order to you. You
will be asked if you consent to the order. The court may not
impose a community sentence without your consent. You
should be aware, however, that if you do not give your consent, the court may be left with no alternative other than a
custodial sentence.

Breaches of Community Orders

If you fail to comply with one or more conditions of an order, you may be brought back to court and the magistrates will consider whether or not the order should be allowed to continue. If they decide that it should, you may have to pay a fine and the term of the order may be extended.

A YOUNG MAN convicted of taking a vehicle without consent and sentenced to a 12-month probation order failed without reasonable excuse to keep three appointments with his probation officer. Brought back to court, he was fined £50 and the length of the order was extended by a further three months. The presiding magistrate told him that if he continued to disregard the terms of the order, he could look forward to a few months in a young offenders' institution instead.

If the court decides to revoke the order, it will substitute a different penalty for the original offence. If you have persistently failed to comply with the requirements of a community order imposed for an offence which is punishable by imprisonment, you are at high risk of being sentenced to a term of imprisonment.

A 22-YEAR-OLD MAN was convicted of causing danger to road users and sentenced to 180 hours' community service. He completed 30 hours but thereafter failed to turn up for work. Brought back to court, the community service order was revoked and he was sentenced to three months' imprisonment for the original offence.

A CUSTODIAL SENTENCE

A magistrates' court is not obliged to impose a custodial sentence for any offence and will only do so if, having considered all other alternatives, the magistrates believe either that the offence is so serious that a term of imprisonment is clearly appropriate or that the offender has not responded to lesser sentences. The maximum terms of imprisonment available to a magistrates' court are:

- 6 months' imprisonment for one offence;

- 12 months' imprisonment for two or more offences.

The risk of a custodial sentence is greatest in one of the following circumstances.

1. Upon conviction for one of the following:

   aggravated vehicle taking;

   causing danger to road users;

   dangerous driving;

   driving while disqualified.

2. Where, upon conviction for any imprisonable offence, the facts reveal considerable aggravating features – for example the offence was committed while the defendant was on bail or there was an obvious attempt to avoid detection or arrest.

3. Where, upon conviction for any imprisonable offence, the facts reveal a particularly serious example of that offence – for example, a conviction for driving with excess alcohol with an extraordinarily high level of alcohol.

4. Where the defendant has a previous conviction or convictions for a similar offence.

The court will, again, ask the probation service to prepare a pre-sentence report and adjourn. You will be told that the court regards the offence as so serious that it has a custodial sentence in mind and it is possible that you will be remanded in **custody** until the next hearing.

A Suspended Prison Sentence

In exceptional circumstances, a prison sentence may be suspended. The effect of, say, six months' imprisonment suspended for two years is that, provided you commit no imprisonable offences during the period of suspension, you will not have to serve the prison sentence.

If, for example, you have commenced work after a long period of unemployment, or if a fresh relationship is having a positive stabilising effect, the court may be persuaded to suspend the term of imprisonment.

Specific Motoring Penalties

In addition to the penalties described above, upon conviction for some offences the court will make one or more of the following orders:

Endorsement of your driving licence with penalty points

For offences which are **endorsable** and the number of penalty points applicable, see Chapter 3.

Key Terms

■ **Custody** A period of detention in either police cells or remand prison ■ **Endorsement** The annotation of your driving licence with penalty points

Upon conviction for most endorsable offences, the number of penalty points which must be ordered is fixed. There are, however, six common offences for which the number of penalty points is variable between a lower and an upper limit at the discretion of the court. These are:

Driving without due care and attention	*3–9*
Using a vehicle without insurance	*6–8*
Driving other than in accordance with a licence	*3–6*
Exceeding the speed limit	*3–6*
Failing to stop after an accident	*5–10*
Failing to report an accident	*5–10*

Having heard the facts of the case and whatever extenuating circumstances you put forward, the magistrates will decide whether the offence is typical of its type, less serious or more serious. Whether you have attended court or simply pleaded **guilty in absence**, you should attempt to influence that decision in the way described in Chapter 10.

There are certain limited circumstances (**special reasons**) in which a court may be persuaded not to endorse your licence at all.

Penalty points remain valid for three years from the date the offence was committed, not from the date on which you were dealt with by a court. (Penalty points for excess alcohol offences are valid for ten years.) If you wish to obtain a clean licence from the DVLA, however, you will have to wait for four years (or 11 years in the case of an alcohol-related offence) from the date that the last endorsable offence was committed.

Key Terms

■ **Guilty in absence** A guilty plea by post or otherwise in the absence of the defendant ■ **Special reasons** Reasons special to the circumstances of the offence which allow a court a discretion not to endorse or not to disqualify

If you are convicted of more than one endorsable offence and these offences were committed at the same time and dealt with on the same occasion, the number of penalty points on your licence will be the highest number ordered for any one offence, not the total number.

A MOTORIST received a summons alleging that he drove without due care and attention and, at the same time and place, he drove with a defective tyre. He pleaded guilty to both charges and they were dealt with on the same day. For driving without due care and attention his licence was endorsed with 6 penalty points and for the defective tyre his licence was endorsed with 3 penalty points.

The effective number of penalty points imposed here is 6, not 9.

When you are convicted of an endorsable offence, the court will keep your licence and return it to you by post, usually within a matter of days. The number of penalty points ordered will be recorded on your licence, together with a code identifying the offence. You are strongly advised to check that the code is correct; mistakes do occur.

A motorist convicted of, for example, failing to provide a roadside specimen of breath, whose driving licence is mistakenly endorsed with the code for refusing specimens for analysis, could have a real problem at any time within the next ten years.

The **endorsement codes** are shown against the offences in Chapters 5 to 8.

Key Terms

■ **Endorsement codes** A code which appears against an endorsement on a driving licence to identify the offences committed

Motorists who accumulate 12 or more penalty points within a three-year period are at high risk of disqualification from driving for six months under the **totting-up** provisions. If, during that three-year period, you have been disqualified from driving for any reason for 56 days or more, the minimum period of disqualification under these provisions becomes 12 months, and for two periods of 56 days or more it becomes two years. You should know, however, that the court has a discretion not to disqualify you at all or to disqualify you for a shorter period if you would face 'exceptional hardship' because of disqualification (see page 200).

Disqualification from Driving

In theory, you may be disqualified upon conviction for any **endorsable** offence. No doubt some unfortunate motorist has been disqualified for having a bald tyre or for driving on the hard shoulder of a motorway. Upon conviction for one of the more serious offences, however, disqualification is obligatory (except if there are **special reasons**). Those offences are:

● aggravated vehicle taking;

● driving with excess alcohol;

● after driving, refusing to give specimens for analysis;

● dangerous driving.

Key Terms

■ **Totting up** The adding together of the number of valid penalty points on your driving licence ■ **Endorsement** The annotation of your driving licence with penalty points ■ **Special reasons** Reasons special to the circumstances of the offence which allow a court a discretion not to endorse or not to disqualify

Upon conviction for one of the above, the court must disqualify you from driving for at least 12 months (unless there are **special reasons**). It makes no difference whatever that disqualification will result in your losing your job, as the court cannot take this into account. An extraordinary number of motorists come to court, plead guilty to driving with excess alcohol and ask the court not to disqualify them because they will lose their job or their wife will divorce them etc. The magistrates must disqualify.

Twelve months is the minimum period of disqualification upon conviction for driving with excess alcohol and is the period of disqualification which would be imposed for a first offence where the level of alcohol is shown to be just over the limit. Magistrates' guidelines include a graph and as the level of alcohol increases, so does the period of disqualification. Disqualification for a first offence of terms of 15 months, 18 months or more is not uncommon.

While you cannot be disqualified for less than 12 months, you should attempt to persuade the court not to disqualify you for any longer than that. Explain why you were drinking and driving. If you drove safely, were not involved in an accident, if you drove only a short distance, make sure the court is aware of that. Tell the court what the effect would be on your job or on your ability to find work if you were disqualified for longer than the statutory minimum. Ask the court to be as lenient as possible.

Key Terms

■ **Special reasons** Reasons special to the circumstances of the offence which allow a court a discretion not to endorse or not to disqualify

Of course, if you were driving having consumed twice or three times the legal limit of alcohol, the court will be thinking in terms of a much longer period of disqualification. Offer an explanation anyway; you have nothing to lose.

Motorists who were driving and, at a police station (or in the case of serious injury, at a hospital), refused to provide samples for analysis, must also be disqualified for a minimum of 12 months. In practice, the court is likely to disqualify for 18 months or more, taking the view that your refusal represents an attempt to evade the consequences of a percentage of alcohol very much higher than the legal limit. If you had some other reason for refusing, what was it? Tell the court.

Second convictions

If you are convicted of an alcohol-related offence (other than failing to provide a roadside breath test), and this is your second such offence within a ten-year period, you must be disqualified for at least three years.

The ten-year period is measured from the date on which you were convicted of the first offence, not from the date you committed it, and the second offence need not be exactly the same as the first.

ON 26 MAY 1984 a motorist was arrested and charged with being in charge of a motor vehicle, having consumed alcohol in excess of the legal limit. He appeared in court on 20 June 1984 and was disqualfied from driving for a period of three months. On 3 June 1994 he was stopped while driving, arrested and taken to a police station where he refused to provide samples for analysis. He was charged with that offence, pleaded guilty and was disqualified from driving for three years.

A motorist convicted of a second offence of dangerous driving within a three-year period must also be disqualified from driving for a minimum of three years (see dangerous driving on page 153).

Interim disqualification

When, after conviction, a court adjourns a case, usually for pre-sentence reports to be prepared, and where disqualification is either obligatory or the magistrates have disqualification in mind, the court may order that you be disqualified from driving until your next court appearance. Special reasons may be argued at this stage.

Interim disqualification is imposed for a specific period which may not be longer than six months, and the period spent under the interim disqualification counts towards whatever period of disqualification the court may order when you are sentenced.

What will happen if you drive while you are disqualified?

When you are disqualified, the presiding magistrate will tell you that the period of disqualification begins at once and that, if you drive during the period of disqualification, you commit an offence for which you may be sent to prison.

A MOTORIST was disqualified from driving for 15 months for driving with excess alcohol. He lived in the country and worked in a city 50 miles away. Before he was disqualified he used to drive to work. During the period of disqualification the only concession he made was to drive each morning as far as the nearest railway station and continue his journey by train. Stopped inevitably by the police, he was charged with driving while disqualified. He pleaded guilty and was sentenced to 56 days' imprisonment.

You may be attending court to plead guilty to an offence for which disqualification is obligatory. You may have been ordered to attend because the magistrates have disqualification in mind either for the offence or under the **totting-up** provisions. An unbelievable number of motorists drive to court in these circumstances and find that they cannot drive home.

One of the aggravating features which may persuade a court to impose a custodial sentence for driving while disqualified is that the defendant drove very soon after his court appearance, after being ordered not to drive.

If there is any possibility of disqualification, do not drive to court unaccompanied.

A MOTORIST was charged with exceeding the speed limit. The **statement of facts** alleged a speed of 75 m.p.h. on a road where speed was restricted to 40 m.p.h. He pleaded guilty in absence but received an **adjournment notice** requiring him to attend for consideration of disqualification for the offence. He attended court, was fined £150 with £30 prosecution costs and was disqualified from driving for 14 days.

Finding himself and his car stranded, he took a chance and drove home. Stopped by the police, he was arrested and brought back before the same court. The magistrates were

---

Key Terms

■ **Totting up** The adding together of the number of valid penalty points on your driving licence ■ **Statement of facts** A document accompanying a summons ■ **Adjournment notice** A notice advising that the case has been adjourned to a particular date

not amused . . . The motorist was sentenced to 28 days' imprisonment and the period of disqualification was increased to three months.

For a fuller account of driving while disqualified see page 79.

Special Reasons for not Disqualifying

These apply to disqualification for the offence, not to disqualification under the **totting-up** provisions.

Just as a court may find **special reasons** for not **endorsing**, there are rare circumstances in which special reasons for not disqualifying may be argued. A special reason is one which is special to the facts of the case, not to the circumstances of the defendant. It must be an extenuating circumstance connected with the commission of the offence and it must not amount to a defence in law.

The fact that disqualification would be too severe a penalty in the circumstances is not a special reason. The fact that the defendant needs a driving licence in the course of his or her employment is not a special reason. Ignorance of the law is not a special reason, neither is it a special reason that the defendant is disabled.

Key Terms

■ **Totting up** The adding together of the number of valid penalty points on your driving licence ■ **Special reasons** Reasons special to the circumstances of the offence which allow a court a discretion not to endorse or not to disqualify ■ **Endorsement** The annotation of your driving licence with penalty points

A MOTORIST was charged with dangerous driving and pleaded guilty. He claimed, however, that he was not aware that a combination of the alcohol he had consumed and the medication he was taking would affect his ability to drive. Special reasons were not found.

Special reasons have been found when a person has consumed alcohol, not intending to drive, but an emergency arises and the person drives. It is necessary, however, to show that the motorist considered all alternatives to deal with the emergency.

A COUPLE stayed overnight in an hotel 70 miles from home. After dinner the wife, who was an epileptic, discovered that she had left her medication at home. Her husband drove home to get her tablets. Stopped and charged with driving with excess alcohol, he pleaded guilty but argued special reasons for not disqualifying. Special reasons were not found.

A DOCTOR who was not on call was nevertheless called out to deal with an emergency. Returning from the call, he was stopped and charged with driving with excess alcohol. The court took the view that the emergency had passed once he had attended his patient and special reasons were not found.

The fact that a motorist drove only a short distance may amount to special reasons.

A MOTORIST who drove his car 200 yards to the nearest car park, and who was then stopped and charged with driving with excess alcohol, argued that the short distance driven amounted to special reasons. The court disagreed.

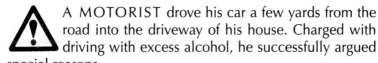 A MOTORIST drove his car a few yards from the road into the driveway of his house. Charged with driving with excess alcohol, he successfully argued special reasons.

In cases where a vehicle is driven only a short distance a court considering special reasons will take into account:

- the distance travelled;
- the manner in which the vehicle was driven;
- the condition of the vehicle;
- whether or not the motorist intended to drive any further;
- the road and traffic conditions;
- the likelihood of danger arising by contact with other road users;
- the reason for driving.

Laced drinks may amount to a special reason for not disqualifying (see page 139).

Finally, you should know that a person who is convicted of a second alcohol-related offence within ten years must be disqualified for at least three years even though, on the first occasion, special reasons for not disqualifying were found.

Discretionary Disqualification

While, in the absence of special reasons, a court must disqualify upon conviction for one of the above offences, you are also at high risk of disqualification from driving in the following circumstances.

1. Under the **totting-up** provisions (see page 214).

Key Terms

■ **Totting up** The adding together of the number of valid penalty points on your driving licence

2. Upon conviction for one of the following offences:

being in charge of a vehicle with excess alcohol;

driving without insurance;

driving in the wrong direction on a motorway;

failing to stop after an accident, particularly if you also failed to report the accident;

taking a vehicle without consent; and

for exceeding the speed limit where the facts reveal that you drove at a speed of 30 m.p.h. or more above the legal limit.

Upon conviction for any of the offences listed above, you are at high risk of disqualification from driving. That is not to say that these are the only offences for which you may be disqualified. The court has the power to disqualify upon conviction for any **endorsable** offence. Some motorists are disqualified, for instance, for driving without due care and attention, but disqualification for this offence would be the exception rather than the rule. The circumstances must have revealed a particularly serious example.

Disqualification for such offences and the period of disqualification is at the discretion of the court.

If, for example, you drive at a speed of 100 m.p.h. or more on a motorway, you will be very fortunate to escape with a mere **endorsement**. But, unless you are driving at some truly ridiculous speed, you may expect the period of disqualification to be measured in weeks rather than months.

Key Terms

■ **Endorsement** The annotation of your driving licence with penalty points

If you use a vehicle without insurance and it is clear to the court that you did so deliberately, i.e. knowing that you were not covered by a policy of insurance, you may expect to be disqualified for a somewhat longer period – and longer still if you have a previous conviction for the same offence. To have any chance of avoiding disqualification for one of the offences where there is a high risk of such a penalty, you must explain the circumstances to the court. Why were you speeding? Why did you fail to stop after an accident? Why were you using a vehicle without insurance?

The court may also take into account the effect of disqualification. A court which has in mind disqualification for 14 days because you were driving at 108 m.p.h. on a motorway is unlikely to be persuaded that such a short period of disqualification will result in your losing your job. On the other hand, a court which has in mind three months' disqualification for being **in charge of** a vehicle with excess alcohol may properly consider the effect of disqualification – it may reduce that period or, if you are very fortunate, may not disqualify you at all.

A fuller account of what you should say and what you should not say is given in Chapter 10. If you can support what you say by documentary evidence – a letter from your employer or, where relevant, from your doctor – so much the better.

Before the Road Traffic Act 1991, even a short period of disqualification had the effect of wiping your licence clean of penalty points. Any valid points on your licence, other than those imposed within the previous ten years for excess alcohol offences, were removed by the disqualification. That is

---

Key Terms

■ **In charge of** A person whose actions fall short of driving but who is shown to be in control of a vehicle

no longer the case. Only a period of disqualification under the **totting-up** provisions now has that effect.

Finally, you should be aware that the effect of even a short period of disqualification is much greater than mere inconvenience. Apart from a temporary increase in the cost of travel, you will find that your insurance premium, assuming that you can obtain insurance, will increase substantially. Worse, if you apply for a job that includes some driving, a would-be employer may well prefer an applicant with a clean licence. . .

AN ORDER FOR A RE-TEST

Upon conviction for any **endorsable** offence, the court may order that you be disqualified until you pass a driving test. Effectively, after the period of disqualification, you become a learner driver until you pass the test. You must display L plates, may not drive unless accompanied by a qualified driver, may not drive on a motorway etc.

The Road Traffic Act 1991 introduced a greater sanction. Upon conviction for certain offences for which disqualification is obligatory, when the period of disqualification expires a driving test is compulsory. This applies mainly to serious motoring offences tried before a judge and jury at a Crown Court, e.g. causing death by dangerous driving, but in the magistrates' court a re-test is compulsory upon conviction for dangerous driving. At the discretion of the court,

---

Key Terms

■ **Totting up** The adding together of the number of valid penalty points on your driving licence ■ **Endorsement** The annotation of your driving licence with penalty points

the test may be either the standard driving test or a more stringent test detailed in the Act.

The penalty upon conviction for dangerous driving thus becomes a possible term of imprisonment, disqualification from driving for at least 12 months and, on the expiry of that period of disqualification, your full licence will not be returned until you have passed the prescribed test.

FORFEITURE OF YOUR VEHICLE

The courts have long had the power to order the forfeiture of a vehicle used in committing a crime. The Road Traffic Act 1991 extended that power so that magistrates' courts may order the forfeiture of your vehicle if you are convicted of any road traffic offence which is punishable by imprisonment.

Motorists, for example, who persistently drive while disqualified are at high risk of losing their vehicle.

Appeals and Applications

APPEALS TO THE CROWN COURT

You have the right to appeal to the Crown Court against the decision of a magistrates' court. You may appeal against a conviction and/or against the sentence imposed.

If you intend to appeal, you or your solicitor must give notice:

1. to the justices' clerk of the sentencing court;

2. to the police;

3. to the Crown Court for the relevant area.

If you have been sentenced to a term of imprisonment and give notice of appeal, you or your solicitor should make an application for **bail** pending the hearing of the appeal. The magistrates, however, are unlikely to allow bail in these circumstances. If the application before the magistrates' court

---

Key Terms

■ **Bail** Release from custody with a duty to surrender to a court at a later date

does fail, your solicitor may apply for bail to a judge in chambers. Such an application is usually heard within 24 hours.

Appeals Against Sentence

Think very carefully before appealing. If you appeal and the appeal is dismissed, you will have to pay a substantial sum in costs. A further point, too, is one which is often overlooked: the judge may impose a more lenient sentence – but he may also impose a more severe sentence.

A MOTORIST had two convictions for driving with excess alcohol, for the second of which he was disqualified from driving for three years. A week or two after his licence was returned, he was charged with failing to provide specimens for analysis. He pleaded guilty and was sentenced to six months' imprisonment and disqualified from driving for three years. He appealed against the sentence.

At the Crown Court, the term of imprisonment was reduced to four months and the period of disqualification was increased to five years.

Appeals Against Conviction

You may only appeal against conviction if you pleaded not guilty before a magistrates' court. Such an appeal is heard before a judge at a Crown Court. Be advised by your solicitor. If you appeal and are again found guilty, you risk a more severe sentence and will be ordered to pay a very substantial sum in costs.

A MOTORIST pleaded not guilty to failing to give precedence to pedestrians on a school crossing. The prosecution alleged that he failed to stop, narrowly missing a lollipop lady and the children she was escorting across the road. The defendant claimed that his vehicle was only a few metres away from the crossing when the lollipop lady stepped out on to the road and that she was at fault.

The motorist was found guilty and, evidently taking an unusually serious view, the magistrates fined him £500, ordered him to pay £120 prosecution costs and disqualified him from driving for six months.

He appealed to the Crown Court against conviction but he was found guilty. The judge fined him £1000 and ordered him to pay the costs of the prosecution. The hapless defendant was disqualified from driving for six months and thereafter until such time as he passed a driving test.

CASES REOPENED

Occasionally, a motorist may be unaware that a summons has been issued against him or her. The motorist may, for example, have changed address or be working abroad. If the person living at the address to which the summons and all the accompanying documents are sent fails to return them to the court or fails to advise the court that the person to whom they are addressed is not there, the prosecution will assume that the documents have been properly served.

When nothing is heard from the defendant, witness statements will be served in the same way and, if these are not returned, the prosecution will ask the court to hear the case in the motorist's absence.

The court will not know that the documents have not been served. A not guilty plea will be entered and the case will be heard. The prosecution will prove its case and the court may proceed to sentence the defendant.

In such cases, you may apply to have the case reopened,

provided you make the application within 28 days of the matter coming to your attention.

⚠ A MOTORIST was working, and temporarily residing, in a distant part of the country. He made no arrangements to have his post forwarded and, returning home after a few months, he found a summons, a number of other documents and a fine notice. The allegation was one of having no MOT certificate. He had an MOT certificate which was valid at the date of the alleged offence. He wrote to the clerk to the justices requesting that the case be reopened.

The case was reopened and the charge was dismissed. The prosecutor advised the court that, in view of the circumstances, she would not proceed with a charge of failing to produce the document.

APPLICATIONS

There are instances where special applications are made to a magistrates' court. The two most common ones are as follows.

An Application by a Disqualified Driver to Have Part of the Disqualification Removed

A person disqualified from driving for a period greater than two years may, after two years have elapsed, apply to the court that imposed the disqualification to have the remaining period of disqualification removed. You must appear in court in person and, if your application is to be successful, you must satisfy the court:

1. that in the intervening two years you have committed no offences

2. that you have a good and adequate reason for the return of your driving licence.

The following may be good and adequate reasons:

• That you are unemployed but have a chance of a job provided your licence is returned. If this is the reason for your application, be sure to support it with documentary evidence – a letter from the proposed employer.

• You have an opportunity for promotion but a driving licence would be necessary. Again, support your application with documentary evidence.

• You live in a rural area and your car is the only means of transport for yourself and your family.

Most commonly, disqualification for more than two years is imposed for an alcohol-related offence. In these circumstances, your application will have a greater chance of success if you demonstrate that you have received treatment for alcohol abuse. Documentary evidence to the effect that treatment was successful and that you no longer drink or now only drink in moderation will improve your chances.

You should write to the court about three months before you intend to make the application. This will usually mean 21 months from the date when the disqualification was imposed.

There is no guarantee that your application will be successful. The court may refuse it, grant it or order that your licence may be restored at a later date, say in three months' time. If your application is refused, you may make another one in three months' time.

One last point: if your application is successful, even though your disqualification may be removed immediately, you will have to apply to the DVLA to get your licence back. Keep a copy of the application, together with evidence that you have paid the fee, because if you do not and you drive, you may be charged with driving otherwise than in accordance with a licence.

An Appeal Against the Decision of the Secretary of State to Remove Your Driving Licence through Ill-Health

The DVLA has the power to remove your driving licence upon receipt of information that you suffer from a condition that renders you unfit to hold such a licence. The various conditions are specified by law and include epilepsy and diabetes. Upon receiving notification that your licence has been removed, you have 21 days in which to appeal.

You should go along to your local magistrates' court and see a court clerk who will help you to fill in the necessary forms, serving a summons on the DVLA and setting a date for the hearing. You will require medical evidence in support of your application. A consultant and/or your general practitioner should either attend court or provide a detailed report.

There is no point whatever in attending court without such a witness or written report because the magistrates will prefer the evidence given by an expert witness on behalf of the DVLA. If your application is successful, the court may order the DVLA to pay your costs, including those of a medical witness or the cost of preparing a report. On the other hand, if the appeal fails, you will be required to pay the costs of the DVLA, including those of its expert witness.

Glossary of Terms

Acquittal The finding of a court that you are not guilty.

Adjournment notice Notice sent by the court informing you that your case has been put off to another date.

Aiding and abetting Helping another in a material way to commit an offence.

Allegation The nature of the offence with which you are charged.

Appeal To have a matter reconsidered by a higher authority, e.g. a Crown Court.

Application Usually to apply to a court for some specific purpose, e.g. for bail or for an adjournment.

Back duty The amount to be paid retrospectively in respect of unpaid vehicle tax.

Bail Your release from custody with a duty to surrender to a court at a later date.

Breach of an order When there is a failure by the defendant to comply with the requirements of an order made by the court.

Breath test A prescribed test performed by a police officer upon a driver suspected of driving while over the legal limit.

Case reopened The facility whereby a magistrates' court can reconsider a case.

Causing Causing another to commit an offence.

Caution The form of words a police officer must use in informing a person of their rights before asking questions.

Charge The offence.

Charged (to be) An alternative way of starting proceedings. Used instead of a summons for more serious offences.

Combination order A sentence combining both a probation order and a community service order.

Committal To be sent by the magistrates to a Crown Court for trial or sentence.

Community sentence   The penalty imposed by a court upon conviction for an offence considered too serious for a fine but not so serious that a custodial sentence is necessary. The most common community sentences are a probation order or a community service order.

Compensation   A sum of money which the court may order you to pay to an injured party.

Conviction   The finding of the court that you are guilty.

Corroboration   Separate and additional evidence that supports or confirms the main evidence.

Costs   A sum of money awarded by the court either to the prosecution or to the defence. The sum awarded represents the cost, or a contribution to the cost, of bringing the matter to court.

Court clerk   The person, usually a barrister or solicitor, who advises magistrates on matters of law and sentence.

Crown Prosecution Service   The service set up by the government to prosecute all criminal offences in the magistrates' courts.

Custodial sentence   A term of imprisonment.

Custody   Period of detention in either police cells or a prison by the order of a court.

Defence   The arguments used when pleading not guilty. The lawyer who represents you.

Defendant   A person charged with an offence.

Disqualification   To be banned from driving.

Duty solicitor   The solicitor available to give advice at court.

Either way offence   An offence which may be tried either before a magistrates' court or before a judge and jury at a Crown Court.

Endorsable offence   An offence upon conviction for which your driving licence will be endorsed with penalty points.

Endorsement   The annotation of your driving licence with penalty points.

Evidence   What is said by witnesses to the court.

Excise licence   The tax disc obtained upon payment of vehicle excise duty.

Extended re-test   The compulsory driving test that has to be passed after a period of disqualification imposed for certain offences.

Fine   The amount imposed as a penalty by the court.

Fixed penalty procedure   The procedure available to avoid a conviction before a court by the payment of a set amount within a stipulated period.

Highway Code   The standard set for all competent drivers to abide by.

HORT I   The notice handed out to drivers by police officers for the production of driving documents to a named police station.

In charge of a vehicle   When a person is shown to be in control of the vehicle but falls short of driving it.

Indictable offence   An offence which may only be tried before a judge and jury at a Crown Court.

Interim disqualification   After conviction for an offence carrying mandatory disqualification but before sentence is imposed, the court can impose disqualification.

Justices   Magistrates.

Justices' clerk   The senior legal adviser to the magistrates.

Legal aid   A scheme whereby financial assistance is given to a person so that he or she may be advised by a solicitor or barrister.

Level of fine   There are five levels of fine which may be imposed by a magistrates' court. Each offence comes within one of these levels.

MOT certificate   Ministry of Transport certificate that must be obtained annually for every vehicle over three years old.

Notice of intention to plead not guilty   A form sent out with the summons by the court which must be returned by the defendant if the plea is not guilty.

Notice of written plea of guilty   A form sent out with the summons by the court which must be returned by the defendant if he or she wishes to plead guilty and have the case disposed of in absence.

Order   A direction by the court, e.g. that you must pay costs.

Penalty points   The points endorsed on your driving licence upon conviction for endorsable offences.

Permitting   Doing some positive act to allow someone else to commit an offence.

Police pilot   A computerised radar system used by the police against speeders.

Probation order   A community-based penalty imposed by the court.

Prosecution The proceedings against you. The lawyer who presents the case against you.

Remand An adjournment, either on bail or in custody.

Sentence The punishment ordered by the court.

Special reasons These apply when the court must disqualify you or must endorse your driving licence and, if they are established, your licence is not endorsed or you are not disqualified or both.

Statement of facts This is a document accompanying the summons sent from the court and sets out brief details of the alleged offence.

Statement of means This is a document accompanying the summons sent from the court. This should be completed and returned if you intend to plead guilty so that the court is aware of your financial circumstances before it decides upon sentence.

Summary offence An offence which may only be tried before a magistrates' court or which may be dealt with by way of a fixed penalty.

Summons The document which begins most prosecutions.

Statement Written evidence.

Suspended sentence A sentence of imprisonment that is not made effective immediately.

Totting up The adding together of all the relevant penalty points on your driving licence.

Trial The process whereby a court hears the evidence from both the prosecution and the defence before reaching a verdict.

VASCAR Visual Average Speed Calculator and Recorder: computerised radar for recording average speed over time and distance travelled.

VDRS Vehicle Defect Rectification Scheme: scheme whereby you are given an opportunity to put right a vehicle defect instead of being prosecuted.

Warrant A document issued by a court, e.g. for your arrest, instructing the police to take you into custody.

Witness A person who saw the alleged incident and who is prepared to give evidence in court.

Common Abbreviations

CPS   The Crown Prosecution Service

DVLA   The Driver Vehicle Licensing Agency, Swansea

HORT 1   The form which requires you to produce your driving documents at a police station

VASCAR   Visual Average Speed Calculator and Recorder

VDRS   Vehicle Defect Rectification Scheme

TABLE OF OFFENCES

Offence	Is it a fixed penalty offence?	What penalty is a court likely to impose	Is the offence endorsable?	Is disqualification likely?	Page number in this book
Summary offences not endorsable					
Carried, allowing yourself to be carried in a vehicle etc.	No	Fine/imprisonment	No	N/A	60
Documents, failing to produce	No	Fine	No	N/A	49
No vehicle excise licence	No	Fine plus back duty	No	N/A	51
Exhaust emission offences	Yes, VDRS possible	Fine	No	N/A	55
Helmet, no safety	Yes	Fine	No	N/A	55
Lighting offences	Yes, VDRS possible	Fine	No	N/A	55
Ownership, not notifying change	Yes	Fine	No	N/A	55
Ownership/driver, failing to supply details of	Yes	Fine	No	N/A	56
Most parking offences	Yes	Fine	No	N/A	55
Seatbelt offences	Yes	Fine	No	N/A	55
Taking a vehicle without consent	No	Community penalty	No	Yes	58
Test certificate, no	No	Fine	No	N/A	62
Summary offences endorsable					
Accident, failing to stop	No	Fine	5–10	Yes	64
Accident, failing to report	No	Fine	5–10	Yes	67
Defective tyre	Yes, VDRS possible	Fine	3	No	70
Double white lines, failing to comply	No	Fine	3	No serious cases	70
Driving without due care	No	Fine	3–11	Only in the most serious cases	73
Driving while disqualified	No	Imprisonment/ community penalty	6	Yes, for a further period	79
Driving not in accordance with a licence	Yes	Fine	3–6	Yes, for unsupervised learner	77
Insurance, using a vehicle without	No	Fine	6–8	Yes, especially if deliberate	83
Leaving in dangerous position	Yes	Fine	3	No	89
Load, insecure	No	Fine	3	No	90
Pedestrian crossing offences	Yes	Fine	3	School crossing, in serious cases	92

Offence					
Speeding, exceeding speed limit	Yes	Fine	3-6	Yes, especially if 30 m.p.h. or more above limit	99
Traffic lights, failing to comply with	Yes	Fine	3	No	105
Police/traffic signs, failing to comply with	Yes	Fine	3	No	105
Using a vehicle in a dangerous condition	Yes, VDRS possible	Fine	3	No	105
Motorway offences					
Exceeding 70 m.p.h.	Yes	Fine	3-6	Yes, at 100 m.p.h. or more	107
Exceeding contraflow speed limit	Yes	Fine	3	Yes, at high speeds	109
Stopping on hard shoulder	Yes	Fine	No	N/A	110
Driving in contravention of traffic sign	Yes	Fine	3	No	117
Driving on hard shoulder	Yes	Fine	3	No	112
Driving in reverse	Yes	Fine	3	No	113
Driving in wrong direction	Yes, but unlikely	Fine	3	Yes	113
Learner driver on motorway	Yes	Fine	3	No	114
Making U-turn	Yes, but unlikely	Fine	3	Yes	115
Unauthorised vehicle in third lane	Yes	Fine	3	No	116
Alcohol-related offences					
Refusing roadside breath test	No	Fine	4	No	125
In charge, with excess alcohol	No	Fine	10	Yes	132
After being in charge, refusing to provide specimens for analysis	No	Fine	10	Yes	136
Driving with excess alcohol	No	Fine	(4)	Compulsory	128
After driving, refusing to provide specimens for analysis	No	Fine	(4)	Compulsory	134
Either way offences before a magistrates' court					
Aggravated vehicle taking	No	Imprisonment	(4)	Compulsory	148
Causing danger to road users	No	Imprisonment	No	N/A	152
Dangerous driving	No	Community penalty/ imprisonment	(6)	Compulsory, compulsory re-test	153
Fraudulent use of excise licence	No	Fine	No	N/A	158

Index

accidents, 23–5, 44, 46, 48, 76, 85,
112, 128, 133; failing to report,
24–5, 65, 67–70, 212, 222, 238;
failing to stop/give particulars, 44,
46, 48, 64–7, 69–70, 212, 222, 238
adjournment, seeking an, 28–9
adjournment notices, 33–4, 79, 98,
101, 178, 182, 193–4, 198,
199–200, 218, 232
aggravated vehicle taking, 144, 148–52,
210, 214, 239
aiding and abetting, 129, 232
Alcohol Offenders Course, 130
alcohol-related offences, 6, 24, 31, 42,
44, 45, 47, 48, 60, 69, 74, 119–43,
165, 212, 214, 215, 216, 217, 220,
221, 222, 227, 230, 239; arrest and
caution, 122, 125, 140; and back
calculations, 130–2; breath tests, 23,
24, 47, 119–21, 122, 123–4, 125–8,
130, 133, 137, 138, 140–1, 239; in
charge of vehicle with excess alcohol,
119, 132–4, 239; driving with excess
alcohol, 119, 128–32; failing to
provide samples for analysis, 47, 48,
119, 123, 124, 134–6, 142, 213,
214, 216, 239; offences, 125–36; at
police station, 122–5, 138, 140–1,
216; procedures, 119–25
alibi warning, 147
ambulance drivers, 75, 157
appeals, 5–6, 111, 226–9, 232; against
conviction, 227–8; against sentence,
227; cases re-opened, 228–9
applications, 5, 6, 229–31, 232; to have
part of disqualification removed, 6,
229–31

arrest and caution, 122, 125, 138,
140–1, 205
automatism (line of defence), 75, 156

back calculations, 130–2
back duty, payment of, 53–4, 55, 166,
232
bail, 5, 34–5, 69, 80, 125, 147, 160,
169, 191, 205, 226, 232; breaking
conditions of, 37, 58, 80; or custody,
35–7
blood samples, 47, 48, 123, 124–5,
130, 134, 136, 141
breath tests, 64, 68, 119–20, 122, 123,
133, 138, 137, 138, 140–1, 232; and
back calculations, 130–2; failing to
provide roadside, 23, 24, 47, 119,
121, 122, 123; other than at
roadside, 121; at police station, 122,
138, 141; random, 121

Camic Breath Analyser, 122
careless and inconsiderate driving, 69–
77, 165; death caused by, 45, 74, 160
cases re-opened, 228–9, 232
causing danger to road users, 144,
152–3, 210, 239
charges, 3, 26, 34–7, 232
clearway, stopping on, 16, 46, 238
Clerk to the Justices, 29, 188, 226
combination order, 4, 130, 207, 208,
232
community penalties, 4, 155, 206–9
community service order, 4, 70, 80,
130, 207–8; breaches of, 209
compensation, 73, 85, 149, 152, 154,
202, 205–6

'consent of the owner', 59
corroboration (of evidence), 102, 110
costs, 172, 202; prosecution, 51, 52, 53, 54, 197, 202, 218, 228
Court Clerk, 28, 170
Criminal Justice Act (1991), 208
Crown Court, 111, 224; alibi warning, 147; appeals to, 5–6, 111, 226–9; either way offences, 4, 144, 145, 146–9, 150, 152, 154, 159, 160; indictable offences, 160; reporting restrictions, 147
Crown Prosecution Service (CPS), 74, 123, 170
custodial sentences, 202, 210–24
custody, remand in, 35–6, 37, 147, 211

damage, 64, 66, 67, 74, 85; compensation for, 205–6
dangerous driving, 44, 45, 47, 144, 153–8, 165, 210, 214, 220, 239; causing death by, 34, 45, 160, 224
defences, 48, 55, 57, 60; alcohol-related offences, 125, 137–43; careless driving, 75–6; contravention of double white lines, 72; driving while disqualified, 81; either way offences, 151, 153, 156–8, 160; exempted vehicles, 52, 53; failing to produce documents, 50; failing to report accident, 68, failing to stop after accident, 66–7; motorway offences, 111, 112, 113, 114, 116, 117; no insurance, 85, 88; specific, 138–9; speeding, 102; taking vehicle, 60; using vehicle without test certificate, 62–3
disabled persons, exemption from excise licence for, 52
discharge, 206; absolute, 202, 203; conditional, 202, 203
disqualification from driving, 5, 20, 24, 42, 58, 65, 70, 74, 178, 189, 192–201, 202, 206, 214–24, 227, 228; alcohol-related offences, 127, 129, 132, 135, 142, 214–16, 217, 220, 221, 222; appeal through ill-health against, 231; application to remove part of, 6, 229–31; attendance at court for consideration of, 192–4; discretionary, 64, 67, 73, 84, 91, 94, 96, 97, 99, 112, 113, 114, 115, 116, 118, 127, 132, 193,

221–4; driving while disqualified, 44, 46, 79–83, 210, 217–19, 238; either-way offences, 149; exceeding speed limit, 195–6, 222, 223, exceptional hardship, 200–1, 214, guilty pleas, 192–201; interim, 217; likelihood of, 45, 48; motorway offences, 107, 108–9, 112, 113, 114, 115–16, 117, 118, 222; obligatory/mandatory, 5, 42, 45, 48, 129, 135, 142, 149, 154, 191, 195, 218; second convictions, 216–17, 221; special reasons for not, 5, 91, 127, 129, 132, 135, 136, 139–40, 141–2, 151, 191, 214, 215, 217, 219–21; under totting-up procedure, 198–200, 218, 219, 221, 224, using vehicle without insurance, 196, 222, 223
distress warrant, 204
double white lines, 46, 70–2; contravention of, 71, 188, 197, 198, 238; stopping on, 70
driving documents, 9–12; failing to produce, 43, 46, 49–50, 63, 101, 183, 185–6, 238
driving licence, 9, 12, 17, 20, 32, 33, 43, 46, 49, 50, 101, 176, 177, 183, 185; provisional, 80; see also endorsement
driving not in accordance with a licence, 77–9, 212, 238; causing or permitting, 79
driving test, 80; extended, 154; order to take retest, 202, 224–5
driving while disqualified, 44, 46, 79–83, 210, 217–19, 238
driving without due care and attention, 46, 74–6, 183, 184–5, 197, 212, 213, 238; see also careless driving
driving without reasonable consideration, 76–7
DVLA (Driver Vehicle Licensing Agency), 9, 12, 17, 33, 50, 53, 55, 159, 166, 177, 183, 186, 212, 231
duty solicitor, 54–5, 69, 77, 81, 92, 98, 103, 142, 163, 165, 168, 191, 200

either way offences, 41, 44, 47, 144–60, 171, 239; aggravated vehicle taking, 144, 148–52, 239; causing danger to road users, 144, 152–3, 239; committal to Crown Court for trial, 146–7, 148; committal for

sentence, 148; dangerous driving,
144, 153–8, 239; fraudulent use of
excise licence, 47, 144, 158–60;
mode of trial procedure for, 145–8;
offences, 148–60; taking vehicle
without consent, 150–2
endorsement (of licence), 2, 5, 15, 16,
17, 20, 22, 31, 33, 34, 41, 43, 45,
46, 154, 172, 176, 185, 191, 197,
202, 206, 211–14, 222, 224; alcohol-
related offences, 126, 128, 132;
motorway offences, 107, 109, 112,
113, 114, 115, 116, 117, 118;
special reasons for not endorsing, 5,
17, 82–3, 88–9, 91, 92, 103, 127,
129, 132, 135, 136, 149, 154,
189–91, 212, 219; summary
offences, 64–105, 238–9
endorsement codes, 65, 213; AC10:
65, 67, AC20: 65; BA10: 80; CD10:
73; CD20: 73; CU50: 91; DD40:
154; DR10: 129; DR30: 135; DR40:
132; DR60: 136; DR70: 126; IN10:
84; LC20: 78; MS10: 89; MW10:
112, 113, 115; PC20: 93, 95, 96;
PC30: 95, 97; SP30: 99; SP50: 107,
SP60: 109; UT50: 149
exceptional hardship, 200–1, 214
excise licence, vehicle, 144, 159, 166;
exempted vehicles, 52–3; fraudulent
use of, 47, 144, 158–60, 239;
maximum penalty, 51; mitigated
penalties, 54; no, 46, 51–5, 238;
payment of back duty, 53–4, 55,
166, 232
exhaust emission offences, 15, 46, 55, 238

fines, 3–4, 17, 23, 31, 32, 42–3, 49,
52, 53, 54, 56, 58, 62, 67, 74, 80,
82, 84, 91, 93, 100, 202, 203–5,
209, 218, 228; alcohol-related
offences, 126, 128, 129, 132, 134;
either-way offences, 149, 152, 154,
158, 159, 160; guilty pleas in
absence, 181, 182, 183, 185–6, 197;
level of, 3, 42–3, 51; maximum, 42;
means of offender, 32–3, 2–3, 2–4;
motorway offences, 107, 109, 110,
112, 113, 114, 115, 116, 117, 118;
seriousness of offence, 203; what will
happen if you don't pay, 204–5
fine default court, 204
fixed penalty, fixed penalty notices, 3, 5,
14, 15–23, 41, 55, 58, 98, 100, 105,
106, 127; affixed to vehicles, 20;
alcohol-related offences, 127, 129,
133, 135, 136; conditional offer, 22;
either-way offences, 149, 152, 154;
endorsable offences, 16, 17, 20, 65,
67, 70, 72, 78, 89, 90, 94, 96, 97, 98,
100, 101, 105; handed to you in
person, 20; motorway offences,
106–7; non-endorsable offences,
15–16, 20; speeding, 183–4, 196;
vehicle defects, 185; what happens if
you do not pay, 23
Fixed Penalty Office, 16, 17, 20, 21,
22, 23, 78, 100
forfeiture of vehicle, 80, 202, 225
'fraudulently', defined, 159

Green Form Scheme, 163
guilty pleas, 4–5, 28, 29, 68, 69, 86,
92, 173–201, 213, 220; attendance
for consideration of disqualification,
192; changing to not guilty pleas, 32,
176; court procedure, 176–8;
disagreeing with statement of facts,
187–9; disqualification for the
offence, 195–201; driving without
due care and attention, 184–5, 197;
exceeding speed limit, 183–4, 195–6,
198; exceptional hardship pleas,
200–1; failing to produce
documents, 185–6; guilty pleas in
person, 187–94; in absence, 4, 29,
52, 54, 56, 58, 63, 65, 67, 72, 73,
76, 79, 86, 89, 90, 91, 92, 94, 96,
97, 98, 101, 108, 127, 133, 154,
173–86, 187, 195, 203, 204, 212; in
general, 183–6; notice of written
(letters to the court), 29, 31, 86,
108, 173, 174, 176, 177, 178–83,
187–8; special reasons for not
endorsing, 189–91; unhelpful
comments, 181–2; using vehicle
without insurance, 196; vehicle
defects, 185; when you are ordered
to attend, 191–2

haemophiliacs, 124
hard shoulder of motorway, driving on,
106, 112, 239; stopping on, 16, 47,
106, 110–11, 239
helmet, no safety, 15, 46, 55, 238
High Court, 123

Highway Code, 2, 90, 117
HORT 1: 9
'hot wired' vehicle, 58

imprisonment, 5, 44–5, 64, 65, 67, 80, 129, 132, 134, 142, 152, 154, 159, 160, 202, 206, 210–24; appeal against, 226; for non-payment of fine, 206; suspended prison sentence, 211
in charge of vehicle offences, 142, 223; failed to provide specimens for analysis, 136; with excess alcohol, 119, 132–4, 223
indictable offences, 41, 45, 160; causing death by careless or dangerous driving, 160; manslaughter, 160
injury, personal, 23, 24, 25, 64, 65, 66, 67, 68, 69, 74, 85, 205, 216
insurance, 9, 12, 24, 32, 43, 46, 48, 49–50, 179, 186, 190–1, 206; causing or permitting, 87–8; driving without, 81, 82, 167; using motor vehicle without, 83–9, 196, 212, 222, 223, 238

L plates, 80–1
Law Society, 164
learner drivers on motorway, 47, 106, 114–15, 239
leaving vehicle in a dangerous condition, 16
leaving vehicle in a dangerous position, 16, 46, 89–90, 133, 238
legal advice, 163–72; duty solicitor scheme, 103, 165, 168; legal aid, 164–7; not guilty pleas, 165–7; procedure before magistrates' court, 169–72
legal aid, 77, 142, 147, 158, 160, 163, 164–7
letters to the court (notice of written guilty pleas), 29, 31, 86, 108, 173, 174, 176, 177, 178, 178–83, 187–8
lighting offences, 15, 46, 55, 238
Lion Intoximeter, 122
load, insecure, 46, 90–2, 238

magistrates' court, 4, 5, 23, 41, 85, 144, 145, 160; appeals against decisions of, 226–8; applications for bail before, 37; applications to,

229–31; disqualification, 193–201; either-way offences before, 41, 47, 144, 145–6, 148, 149, 152, 154, 155, 159, 160, 239; guilty pleas in absence, 173–83; notice of adjournment, 33–4, 79, 98, 101, 178, 182, 193–4, 198–200, 218; procedure before, 169–72; sentences and orders, 202–25; summary offences before, 41; summons to appear before, 26–34
manslaughter, 45, 160
means form, 142
mistaken identity, 60, 81, 102, 137, 151
MOT certificate, 9, 12, 32, 42, 43, 46, 49–50, 52, 54, 167, 238
motorway offences, 47, 81, 106–18, 239; driving in contravention of traffic signs, 106, 117–18, 239; driving in reverse, 47, 106, 113–14, 239; driving in wrong direction, 47, 48, 106, 113–14, 222, 239; driving on central reservation or hard shoulder, 106, 112, 239; driving unauthorised vehicle in third lane, 47, 106, 116–17, 239; exceeding contraflow speed limit, 47, 57, 106, 109–10; exceeding speed limit, 106, 107–9; learner driver on, 47, 106, 114–15, 239; making U turn, 47, 48, 106, 115–16, 239; stopping on hard shoulder, 16, 47, 106, 110–11, 239
Motorway Traffic (Speed Limit) Regulations (1974), Regulation 3: 107

not endorsable offences, summary, 46, 49–63, 238
not guilty pleas, 4, 31, 54–5, 63, 165–7, 171; notice of intention, 31, 167
'notice to the owner', 21

ownership, 16; failure to notify change of, 16, 46, 55, 56–7, 238

Panda cars, 102, 103, 188–9
paper committal, 146
parking offences, 16, 46, 55, 57, 238
pedestrian crossing offences, 16, 46, 92–8, 238; pelican crossings, 94–6; school crossing, 97–8, 227–8; zebra crossing, 92–4
Pelican Crossing Regulations and General Directions (1987), 95, 96

Pelican Crossings, 94–6; failing to give precedence to pedestrian, 95, 96; failing to stop when red light is showing, 94–5; overtaking within limits, 95, 96; stopping in area adjacent to, 96; waiting within limits, 95

penalties, 202–25; compensation, 73, 85, 149, 152, 154, 205–6; community, 4, 70, 80, 130, 155, 206–9; custodial sentence, 202, 210–24; forfeiture of vehicle, 80, 202, 225; likely, 41, 42–8; mitigated, 53; order for re-test, 202, 224–5; other than fines, 44–8; probation orders, 4, 80, 129–30; specific motoring, 211–14; see also disqualification; endorsement; fixed penalty; imprisonment; penalties, maximum

penalties, maximum, 48; alcohol-related offences, 126–7, 129–30, 132, 134–5, 136; careless and inconsiderate driving, 73; contravention of double white lines, 71–2; dangerous driving, 154–6; driving not in accordance with licence, 77–8; driving while disqualified, 80–1: either-way offences, 149–50, 154–6, 159; failure to produce documents, 49–50; failure to stop/report accidents, 64–6, 67–8; failure to supply details of ownership, 56–7; insesure load, 91; leaving vehicle in dangerous position, 89–90; motorway offences, 107, 109, 110–11, 112, 113, 114, 115–16, 118; no excise licence, 51; no insurance, 84–5; pedestrian crossing offences, 93–4, 96, 97–8; speeding, 99; taking vehicle without consent, 58–9; using vehicle without test certificate, 62

penalty points, 17, 20, 31, 41, 43, 64, 67, 78, 80, 82, 91, 181–2, 211–14; totting up, 5, 20, 48, 82, 189, 192, 194, 198–200, 214, 218, 219, 221, 224; see also endorsement

Police Enquiries Book, 50

police pilot, 102

police station, alcohol-related offenders at, 122–5, 138, 140–1, 216

police/traffic signs, failing to comply with, 16, 47, 105, 239

press/newspapers, 170

probation order, 4, 80, 129-30, 207, 209

Probation Service, pre-sentence report by, 206–7

prosecution, 26, 28, 29, 31, 33, 48, 58–9, 63, 66, 73, 75, 80, 81, 135, 145, 146, 167, 170, 171, 188, 227; costs of, 51, 52, 53, 54, 197, 202, 218, 228

random searches by police, 9

reasonable excuse, 127, 135, 136

registration number of vehicle, 23, 28

reverse driving on motorway, 47, 106, 113–14, 239

Road Traffic Act (1920), 62

Road Traffic Act (1988), Part 3: 79; Part 6: 83; Schedule 2: 153; section 2: 153; section 3: 73; section 5: 132; section 5(a) (a), 128; section 6(4), 126; section 7: 134, 136; section 22: 89; section 22A: 152; section 36: 70, 71; section 40A: 91; section 47: 62; section 87: 77; section 103: 79; section 143: 83; section 165(1), 49; section 170(4), 64, 67; section 172(2), 56

Road Traffic Act (1991), 65, 199, 223, 224–5; Schedule 4: 89

Road Traffic (Consequential Provisions) Act (1988), Schedule 2: 62

Road Traffic Offenders Act (1988), Scheule 2: 64, 67, 92, 95, 97

Road Traffic Regulation Act (1984), section 6: 99; section 14: 56; section 15: 115; section 17(4), 110, 112, 113, 114, 116, 117; section 25(5), 92, 95; section 28(3), 97; section 81: 99; section 84: 99; section 88: 109; section 89: 99; section 112(4), 56

Road Vehicles Construction and Use Regulations (1986), Regulation 100: 91

School Crossings, 97–8, 227–8

seatbelt offences, 16, 20, 42, 46, 55, 238

sentences and orders, 202–25; apeals against, 226–7; cases re-opened, 228–9; community penalties, 206–9; compensation, 205–6; custodial sentences, 210–24; dischange, 203;

sentences and orders – *contd*
fines, 203–5; forfeiture of vehicle, 225; order for re-test, 224–5; *see also* penalties
solicitors, 3, 4, 28, 29, 31, 34, 35, 36, 37, 69, 77, 81, 83, 92, 142, 144, 145, 158, 160, 163, 164–5, 181, 191, 226, 227; duty, 54–5, 69, 77, 81, 92, 98, 103, 142, 163, 165, 168, 191, 200
special reasons for not endorsing or disqualifying, 5, 17, 82–3, 88–9, 91, 92, 103, 127, 129, 132, 135, 136, 139–40, 141–2, 149, 151, 154, 187, 189–91, 212, 214, 215, 217, 219–21
specimens/samples for analysis, failing to provide, 44, 45, 47, 48, 123, 124–5, 128, 130, 138–9, 141, 142, 213, 214, 216; after being in charge, 119, 136, 239; after driving, 119, 134–5, 239; and back calculations, 130–2
speeding, exceeding speed limit, 16, 20, 28, 31, 47, 48, 74, 99–104, 166, 212, 239; corroboration of evidence, 102; defences, 102; disqualification, 195–6, 218, 222, 223; exempted vehicles, 102, 104; guilty pleas, 183–4, 188–9, 195–6, 198; inciting the commission of offence, 104; maximum penalty, 99; motorway, 106, 107–9, 239; motorway contraflow system, 47, 57, 106, 109–10, 239; recorded on camera, 57; special reasons for not endorsing, 103
statement of facts, statutory, 21, 23, 29, 30, 176, 177, 180, 187, 218; disagreeing with, 187–9
statements of means, 32–3, 204
statement of ownership, 21, 23
summary offences, 41, 44, 46–7, 146; endorsable, 46–7, 64–105, 238–9; not endorsable, 46, 49–63, 238
summons, 3, 4, 14, 15, 17, 26–34, 40, 54, 63, 195, 197, 169, 173–6, 185, 186, 196, 228; what will happen if you ignore, 33–4

Temporary Speed Limits Order (1977), sub-section (1)(b), 109
test certificate *see* MOT certificate
Theft Act (1968), section 12A, 149
'to forge', defined, 159
totting up provisions, 5, 20, 48, 82, 189, 192, 194, 214; disqualification under, 198–200, 214, 218, 219, 221, 224
trade licence place holders, 52
traffit lights, failing to comply with, 16, 47, 105, 106, 117–18, 197, 239
traffic patrol cars, 102
traffic wardens, 16, 21
trailers, 65, 67, 89, 117
tyres, defenctive, 16, 46, 70, 213, 238

Unit Fine system, 204
urine samples, 124–5, 130, 134, 136, 138–9, 141; *see also* specimens for analysis
using a vehicle in a dangerous condition, 105, 239
U-turn, making on motorway, 47, 48, 106, 115–16, 239

Vascar, 102
VDRS (Vehicle Defect Rectification Scheme), 12–15, 41, 55, 70, 105, 185
vehicle condition, 12–15, 47, 183
vehicle taking without consent, 44, 46, 48, 58–60, 209, 222, 238; aggravated, 44, 45, 47; allowing yourself to be carried in, 60–61; 'consent of the owner', 59, 60; defences, 60, 61; 'for your use or that of another', 59; 'lawful authority', 59, 60; maximum penalty, 58–9, 61
Vehicles (Excise) Act (1971), section 81, 51; section 26(1)(c), 158

Zebra Crossings, 92–4; failing to give precedence, 92, 94, 96; overtaking within limits, 93, 94; stopping in area adjacent to crossing, 93; waiting withing the limits, 93, 94
'Zebra' Pedestrian Crossing Regulations (1871), 9(1), 93; 8: 92; 10: 93; 12(2), 93